Anti-Asian Racism

Myths, Stereotypes, and
Catholic Social Teaching

Anti-Asian Racism

Myths, Stereotypes, and
Catholic Social Teaching

Joseph Cheah

ORBIS BOOKS
Maryknoll, New York 10545

Founded in 1970, Orbis Books endeavors to publish works that enlighten the mind, nourish the spirit, and challenge the conscience. The publishing arm of the Maryknoll Fathers and Brothers, Orbis seeks to explore the global dimensions of the Christian faith and mission, to invite dialogue with diverse cultures and religious traditions, and to serve the cause of reconciliation and peace. The books published reflect the views of their authors and do not represent the official position of the Maryknoll Society. To learn more about Maryknoll and Orbis Books, please visit our website at www.orbisbooks.com

Library of Congress Cataloging-in-Publication Data

Names: Cheah, Joseph, author.
Title: Anti-Asian racism : myths, stereotypes, and Catholic social teaching / Joseph Cheah.
Description: Maryknoll, New York : Orbis Books, [2023] | Includes bibliographical references and index. | Summary: "An up-to-date analysis of anti-Asian racism, from a Catholic perspective"— Provided by publisher.
Identifiers: LCCN 2022026625 (print) | LCCN 2022026626 (ebook) | ISBN 9781626984790 (trade paperback) | ISBN 9781608339419 (epub)
Subjects: LCSH: Asian Americans—Civil rights. | Racism--United States. | United States—Race relations. | Racism—Religious aspects—Catholic Church. | Christianity and culture—Moral and ethical aspects—United States.
Classification: LCC E184.A75 C483 2023 (print) | LCC E184.A75 (ebook) | DDC 305.895/073--dc23/eng/20220615
LC record available at https://lccn.loc.gov/2022026625
LC ebook record available at https://lccn.loc.gov/2022026626

To my mom, who remains for me the person who most clearly mirrors God's unwavering love and care.

CONTENTS

INTRODUCTION

In an effort to address the evil of racism and its harmful effects, the US Conference of Catholic Bishops (USCCB) issued a pastoral letter, *Open Wide Our Hearts: The Enduring Call to Love—A Pastoral Letter Against Racism*, in its November 2018 General Assembly. This was a long overdue pastoral statement on racism, released four decades after the 1979 pastoral letter *Brothers and Sisters to Us: A Pastoral Letter on Racism in Our Day,* and sixty years after the 1958 statement on *Discrimination and Christian Conscience.* In *Open Wide Our Hearts*, the bishops continued not only the theme of the sinful nature of racism and its violation of the fundamental dignity of the human person, discussed in their previous pastoral letter on racism, but also recognized the Church's failure to reckon with racial injustice over centuries in the Americas.[1]

Open Wide Our Hearts is an improvement over previous pastoral statements in its acknowledgment of the Church's complicity in the evil of racism. However, as a pastoral letter against racism, it has rendered the struggles and racialized experiences of Asian Americans and Pacific Islanders (AAPI) completely invisible. This in part has to do with how the Catholic Church in the United States reflects the larger American society in the ways in which the AAPI are relegated as foreigners or outsiders in their own country and, consequently, their experiences become either subordinated or have been consis-

---

[1] US Conference of Catholic Bishops, *Open Wide Our Hearts: The Enduring Call to Love—A Pastoral Letter Against Racism* (Washington, DC: USCCB, 2018), 17–18.

tently excluded in the mainstream American history, pastoral letters, and political discourses. This has contributed to the invisibility of AAPI experiences of pain and suffering, xenophobia, and racism in racial discourses in academia, the entertainment industry, and in the Church. Not too many Americans know about the horrific violence and racism suffered by Asian immigrants in the past, and few non-AAPI Americans would take seriously racism and discrimination experienced by AAPI prior to the COVID-19 pandemic.

Despite the spike in violence in the Asian American community during this pandemic, a recent survey conducted by LAAUNCH (Leading Asian Americans to Unite for Change) reveals that 37 percent of White Americans are not aware of a surge in anti-Asian hate violence and 24 percent of White Americans do not believe that Asian Americans suffer from racism.[2]

In 2018, the USCCB promulgated not only *Open Wide Our Hearts* but also a pastoral response about AAPI or Asian and Pacific Islanders, *Encountering Christ in Harmony: A Pastoral Response to Our Asian and Pacific Island Brothers and Sisters.* The latter presents AAPI in terms of their identity, generations, leadership, cultural encounter, and dialogue in faith. In addition, *Encountering Christ in Harmony* attempts to respond to racism experienced by AAPI in stating that racism based on language and physical appearance "can sometimes be negative due to racism" and that AAPI are "sometimes portrayed" as "model minorities." The use of such conditional phrasings trivializes racism experienced by AAPI as if it is not widespread or systemic.[3] While the drafter correctly brought up the

---

[2] Leading Asian Americans to Unite for Change (LAAUNCH), "Survey Reveals 8 out of 10 Asian Americans Say They Are Discriminated Against and 77% Do Not Feel Respected in the U.S.," *Associated Press News*, May 10, 2021.

[3] US Conference of Catholic Bishops, *Encountering Christ in Harmony: A Pastoral Response to Our Asian and Pacific Island Brothers and Sisters* (Washington, DC: USCCB, 2018), 18–20.

idea that the model minority myth has made AAPI invisible in the politics of US racial discourses,[4] a discussion of such a complicated myth like the model minority, in passing, without mentioning the ideology of White supremacy that made the model minority trope possible, is entirely inadequate.

In a fifty-eight–page booklet, it spent a seemingly obligatory amount of time—slightly over a page—addressing racism experienced by Asians and Pacific Islanders in the United States, plus four sidebars about racism from the 1979 pastoral letter. The largest of these sidebars provides a definition of racism from the previous pastoral letter and a quote from the late Cardinal Francis George on racism. The other three sidebars are synopses of the previous pastoral letter's response to racism from personal, Christian, and parish levels. No reference was made to any of the works done by Asian American scholars and theologians on race/racism, Asian American history, experience, and theology.

The document recognizes the role of social structures in reinforcing racism by identifying two disconcerting events in US history. However, it does so in passing or essentializing Asian American history into the worst form of tokenism: mentioning the 1882 Chinese Exclusion Act and the incarceration of Japanese Americans during World War II within the same sentence while providing neither context nor sufficient explanation. The sentence reads, "While the experience of racism is not unique to any one ethnic group, two important examples in Asian American history include the Chinese Exclusion Act in 1882 and the internment of Japanese Americans during the Second World War."[5] What is troubling about this is that not only is the group that had the power to enact the 1882 Chinese Exclusion Act and the incarceration of Japanese Americans made nameless, but the conditional phrasing

---

[4] Ibid., 19.
[5] Ibid., 18.

of the sentence trivializes these two horrific events in the history of Asian Americans as a consequence of ordinary racism. Furthermore, the entire section on racism was written in passive voice, except for when the drafter writes about interethnic discriminations between Asian and Pacific Islanders and how they contribute to the racial discourse in the United States. Instead of focusing on the virulent form of racism that resulted in the Chinese Exclusion Act and the incarceration of Japanese Americans, the drafter diverts the attention to interethnic tensions that can be found in almost all groups, especially in a very broad umbrella group like the AAPI.

The big elephant in the room remains: the ideology of Whiteness and White supremacy, which are completely omitted in the document. It is obvious that *Encountering Christ in Harmony* is a compensative product of a committee that attempts to engage in the topic of racism because the racialized experience of AAPI was excluded in *Open Wide Our Hearts*.

This book thus fills a large lacuna in the Catholic Church's understanding and treatment of the racialized experiences of AAPIs. It focuses on the central issue that the bishops' documents do not address, namely, reckoning with the invisibility of AAPI in the church. As a vital part of the ongoing conversation on racial reckoning in the church and country, this volume approaches racism and xenophobia experienced by Asian Americans systematically by examining three destructive and pervasive stereotypes that have negatively shaped the lives of AAPI in general and Asian Americans in particular: yellow peril, the model minority, and the perpetual foreigner. I examine these three damaging stereotypes from the perspectives of history, Asian American Studies, Asian American marginal theology, biblical studies, and Catholic Social Teaching (CST). In addition, I periodically employ the bishops' pastoral letter, pastoral response, and papal encyclicals in my discussion. As such, this book supplements the discussion of race/racism in *Open Wide Our Hearts* and *Encountering Christ in Harmony* by offering a response to issues of racial injustice confronted by AAPI communities.

Before describing the organization of this book, some introduction to terms and concepts is in order.

Race, Racism, and the Pastoral Letter

Race, racism, and White supremacy are some of the central concepts running through this volume. Race is not a biological reality, but rather a social construction with real socioracial effect. Race is a set of beliefs and practices that gives meaning to the perception of phenotypic differences as essential, and how those perceived essential differences become markers of social and cultural inequality.[6] In other words, race speaks the language of phenotype, but it is really about the social power exercised by the dominant group over targeted racial groups with relatively less social power in the United States.

According to the 1979 bishops' pastoral letter, *Brothers and Sisters to Us*, racism is "a sin that divides the human family, . . . and violates the fundamental human dignity of those called to be children of the same Father. Racism is the sin that says some human beings are inherently superior and others essentially inferior because of races."[7] The strength in the first part of this definition is that it makes clear that racism, in all manifestations, is a sin because it violates the fundamental dignity of every human being. A weakness in the second part of this definition is the use of passive voice. It is not a good idea to define racism in terms of generic "races" when race as a categorizing term in reference to human beings first emerged in sixteenth-century Europe, and

---

[6] Joseph Cheah, *Race and Religion in American Buddhism: White Supremacy and Immigrant Adaptation* (New York: Oxford University Press, 2011), 22.

[7] US Conference of Catholic Bishops, *Brothers and Sister to Us: U.S. Bishops' Pastoral Letter on Racism in Our Day* (Washington, DC: USCCB, 1979).

by the eighteenth century, it formed a racialized social structure "that awarded systemic privileges to Europeans (the peoples who became "white") over non-Europeans (the peoples who became "nonwhite").[8] This racialized social system is the earliest formulation of White supremacy. While this term seems to cause knee-jerk reactions in many bishops of the USCCB, it is quite appropriate to use it in a document promulgated in part to respond to the resurgence of White nationalism in Charlottesville in 2017. Not only is "White nationalism" not mentioned in the pastoral letter, even the term "White privilege," as Sister of Mercy Karen M. Donahue noted, is conspicuously missing in the bishops' pastoral letters and response.[9]

In her honest appraisal of the 2018 pastoral letter, Mary T. Yelenick, a member of the Pax Christi USA Anti-Racism Team, underscores that "the document will necessarily remain unrepresentative, unfinished, and unhelpful" because while the experiences of Native Americans, African Americans, and Hispanics are briefly discussed in the pastoral letter, the voices of the people from those communities, as well as the voices of theologians and other scholars who have spent their careers writing about racism in these communities and in the Catholic Church, are missing. She also noted that the document "does not acknowledge, address, or seek atonement for the unique role of the Catholic Church in perpetuating and practicing racism."[10]

In his interview with the *National Catholic Reporter*, Father Bryan Massingale of Fordham University pointed out that when

---

[8] Bonilla-Silva, *Racism without Racists: Color-Blind Racism and the Persistence of Racial Inequality in America* (Lanham, MD: Rowman & Littlefield, 2018), 8.

[9] Sister Karen M. Donahue, "*Open Wide Our Hearts*—What I Wish the Bishops Would Have Said," Sisters of Mercy.org, January 21, 2019.

[10] Mary T. Yelenick, "An Anti-Racism Perspective on *Open Wide Our Hearts*, the November 2018 Bishops' Pastoral Letter on Racism," Pax Christi USA, October 31, 2019.

the document refers to racism it does so in the passive voice.[11] We see this in the first sentence under "The African American Experience," which reads, "As this country was forming, Africans were bought and sold as mere property, often beaten, raped, and literally worked to death."[12] Who bought and sold Africans as mere property, literally working them to death? This is not an isolated example. Most of the document was written this way. As Massingale puts it candidly: "The document was written by white people for the comfort of white people. And in doing so, it illustrates a basic tenet of Catholic engagement with racism: when the Catholic Church historically has engaged this issue, it's always done so in a way that's calculated to not disturb white people or not to make white people uncomfortable."[13] Daniel P. Horan, professor of theology at St. Mary's College in Notre Dame, Indiana, echoes Massingale's point by challenging the US bishops to leave their comfort zone and acknowledge "the basic truth that racism is a white problem and progress will only be made when church leaders accept and preach this fact."[14] All these reviewers called out the Church for its lack of acknowledgment of White privilege and White supremacy. They consider the pastoral letter to be ineffective because it "hides behind lofty rhetoric to avoid dealing with uncomfortable truths,"[15] "was written in passive voice,"[16] never mentioned White privilege,[17] and "never names the sinner."[18]

[11] Regina Munch, "An Interview with Bryan Massingale: 'Worship of a False God,'" *NCR*, December 27, 2020.

[12] USCCB, *Open Wide Our Hearts*, 10.

[13] Munch, "An Interview with Bryan Massingale."

[14] Daniel P. Horan, "When Will the US Bishops Address the Evil of Systemic Racism Head-on?" *NCR*, June 10, 2020.

[15] Yelenick, "An Anti-Racism Perspective."

[16] Munch, "An Interview with Bryan Massingale."

[17] Donahue, "*Open Wide Our Hearts*."

[18] Horan, "When Will the US Bishops Address the Evil of Systemic Racism Head-on?"

Despite its weaknesses, the general principle or scriptural passage referred to in the pastoral letter can be used to frame the discussion of a topic not directly mentioned in the letter itself. For example, the writer of the educational resource "Examining Our Subconscious Perception," which is accessible at the USCCB website, took a general statement from the pastoral letter that "[r]acism can often be found in our hearts—in many cases placed there unwillingly or unknowingly by our upbringing and culture"[19] and related it to an implicit bias experienced by Asian Americans in particular. Even though the writer did not name the ethnic group, the phrase, "the common stereotype that certain groups are smart and serious,"[20] is usually attributed to Asian Americans. This is a general statement that could have been applied to any racial/ethnic group, but the writer is using it in relation to Asian Americans because of their reference to certain groups as "smart and serious" followed by an example of a person "good at math," which is another common stereotype ascribed to Asian Americans. As the writer puts it, "For example, if it is assumed that one person is 'good at math' because of his or her background, could that assumption preclude opportunities for work in a more creative field? Stereotypes, even when they seem complimentary, are never good because they do not honor people as individuals, created by God, with unique gifts and talents."[21] The writer's point is well taken that even seemingly "good" stereotypes can channel, in this case, Asian Americans to the STEM (science, technology, engineering, and mathematics) field. This is a good example of how a general statement or scriptural passage referenced in a pastoral letter can be used to apply to situations not directly mentioned and, perhaps, not explicitly intended, in the pastoral letter itself.

---

[19] USCCB, *Open Wide Our Hearts*, 5.

[20] US Conference of Catholic Bishops, *Examining Our Subconscious Perception* (Washington, DC: USCCB, 2022), 2.

[21] Ibid.

Catholic Social Teaching

CST is a body of teaching on social, economic, and political life from the magisterium of the Church, based on the fundamental principles of the Catholic social doctrine: the Dignity of the Human Person, the Common Good, Subsidiarity, and Solidarity. These are principles listed by the Pontifical Council for Justice and Peace in its 2004 doctrinal corpus overview, *Compendium of the Social Doctrine of the Church.*

The USCCB summarizes the CST into seven basic principles: Life and Dignity of the Human Person; Call to Family, Community, and Participation; Rights and Responsibilities; Option for the Poor and Vulnerable; The Dignity of Work and the Rights of Workers; Solidarity; and Care for God's Creation.[22] Different Catholic organizations and applications have slightly different permutations of the principles, but they all begin with the foundational principle of the Dignity of the Human Person, because Christians believe that all humans are created in the image and likeness of God.

While the modern history of CST began with the publication of Pope Leo XIII's *Rerum Novarum* in 1891, CST draws upon sources as old as Scripture itself. The first creation story in the book of Genesis is often referenced to support the dignity of the human person. In Genesis 1, God (*Elohim*), out of the dark chaos and formless void, created the heavens and the earth and all living things in six days. On the first day, as the wind of God swept over the waters, God names light and darkness "day" and "night." On the second day, God inserts an immense dome to separate "the water above the dome from the water below it" (Gn 1:8). On the third day, God brings forth vegetation of every kind and fruit trees with seed-bearing fruit. On the fourth day, God makes the sun to

---

[22] Bernard V. Brady, *Essential Catholic Social Thought* (Maryknoll, NY: Orbis Books, 2008), 11–15.

govern the day and the moon to govern the night. On the fifth day, God makes the living creatures in the sea and the birds that fly in the sky. On the sixth day, God brings forth all kinds of living creatures that roam the earth, and the climatic event on that day is the creation of human beings. Unlike the plants, fishes, birds, and other animals, human beings are created in the image and likeness of God.[23]

The fundamental principle of the dignity of the human person in the CST is based on this passage in Genesis (Gn 1:27). Human beings are sacred because we are created in the image and likeness of God. In nonscriptural language, this is written as the dignity of the human person. Both sacredness and dignity of the human person is at the heart of CST. Respect and dignity are fundamental God-given rights. This is based neither on an individual's merits nor on one's race, ethnicity, culture, sexuality, or other personal attributes. Respect and dignity require no other rationale than that these are gifts from God.

In the Old Testament, the book of Genesis tells us that human beings are sacred because we are created in the image and likeness of God. In the New Testament, God takes the sacredness of humans to a new level by becoming one of us in Christ. The Incarnation is a message from God who draws near to us and says, "You are bone of my bones and flesh of my flesh" (Gn 2:23). We have common roots with God. The Incarnation tells us that humans matter because our humanity is consecrated by the birth of Christ. In a sense, humans are doubly sacred. Not only are we created in the image and likeness of God, but we are also consecrated by the birth of Jesus. This is why the respect for the dignity of the human person is the paramount principle of CST.

---

[23] Raymond E. Brown, Joseph A. Fitzmyer, and Ronald E. Murphy, *The New Jerome Biblical Commentary* (Hoboken, NJ: Prentice Hall, 1990), 10–11.

Whiteness and White Supremacy

A final set of concepts to introduce and define before we begin, are these.

Whiteness as a legal construction can be traced back to the 1790 Naturalization Act, which restricted admission into the American national community to "free white persons." Because "whiteness" or "white persons" was not clearly defined in the act, the Supreme Court judges appealed to "scientific evidence" and "common knowledge" to determine whether the applicant belonged to the "white" race. The enforcement of this act was full of ambiguity as the court, on the basis of their rulings, had difficulty making consistent decisions.

Two famous racial prerequisite cases illustrate this ambiguity and contradiction. Takao Ozawa, an immigrant from Japan, graduated from the University of California at Berkeley and eventually settled in the territory of Hawaii with his family. At a time when Asians were looked upon as unassimilable, Ozawa was one of the most assimilated immigrants in the United States. He converted to Christianity, lived the American lifestyle, and raised his children to speak only English at home. In 1922, he petitioned to the US Supreme Court to grant him citizenship. The Court rejected Ozawa's application by declaring that he was not "popularly known as the Caucasian race" and that he was of a Mongoloid race, thus invoking both common knowledge and accepted science at that time.[24] A few months later, Bhagat Singh Thind, a South Asian man, applied for citizenship based on the argument that Western anthropologists classified Asian Indians as "Caucasians" rather than "Mongolians." The Supreme Court contradicted its ruling of Ozawa by rejecting the prevailing race science of the time that

---

[24] Ian F. Haney Lopez, *White by Law: The Legal Construction of Race* (New York: New York University Press, 1996), 7.

categorized Thind as racially White; instead, they privileged the common knowledge argument that Thind would not be considered White in the eyes of most people. Moreover, the purity of his genealogical claims of Caucacian and Aryan ancestry depended on his religion. Although Thind was a Sikh, the Court rejected his citizenship application on the basis of his "Hindooism."[25] Hence, the legal and social category of Whiteness was an unstable identity category, subject to inclusion and exclusion based on the biases of the judges.

In 1790, southern and eastern Europeans would not be considered White but, by the 1920s, they could be White for purposes of naturalization, even though they were still considered to be racially inferiors to Anglo-Saxons.[26] In other words, White people were not a natural group, but were socially and legally constructed. This concept of Whiteness as it emerged in the courts in their interpretation of the 1790 Naturalization Act is a classic example of White supremacy: the idea that "European," which served as a synonym for Whites, was privileged in the naturalization process and assumed to be inherently superior to non-White Others in the construction of the American national identity.

Among racial theorists and social reformers of the early twentieth century who claimed that Whiteness had biological and scientific foundation were Madison Grant and Lothrop Stoddard. Both made the racist assertion that reflected the racially biased eugenics of the time: there were naturalized hierarchies of distinction among different races, with Whites on the apex of all these hierarchies. Furthermore, they warned that the hegemony of the

---

[25] Jennifer Snow, "The Civilization of White Man: The Race of the Hindu in United States v. Bhagat Singh Thind," in Henry Goldschmidt and Elizabeth McAlister, eds., *Race, Nation, and Religion in the Americas* (New York: Oxford University Press, 2004), 261–80.

[26] Ibid., 104, 106.

White race was being threatened by the growing population of "colored people" in the United States and around the world. Grant drew upon nineteenth-century French thinking on race with its tripartite division of European racial typology—Alpine, Mediterranean, and Nordic—and claimed that the Nordic were the superior race among Whites and argued for the preservation and flourishing of Nordic supremacy through eugenic programs and immigration restrictions.[27] Like Grant, Stoddard foresaw the downfall of Western civilization from the rapid growth of "colored" masses, which he artificially categorized into "yellows, blacks, browns, and reds."[28] The writings of both Grant and Stoddard were influential in the conceptions of Whiteness and White supremacy during the period when social Darwinist and eugenist conceptions of race were prominent in Europe and America. For them, Whiteness had biological and scientific foundations. They did not equivocate in saying that the White race was superior to all others. The rationale for the enslavement of African Americans and the exclusion of Chinese came from these assumptions.

Two definitions of White supremacy that best describe these oppressive situations are offered by George Frederickson, who refers to "the attitudes, ideologies, and policies" associated with the rise of blatant forms of White or European dominance over non-Whites,[29] and Robin DiAngelo, who posits "the definition of whites as the norm or standard for human, and people of color as a deviation from that norm."[30] Today, no reputable person

---

[27] Madison Grant, *The Passing of the Great Race* (New York: Charles Scribner's Sons, 1916), 20–28.

[28] Lothrop Stoddard, *The Rising Tide of Color against White World Supremacy* (New York: Charles Scribner's Sons, 1922), 3–10.

[29] George Frederickson, *White Supremacy: A Comparative Study of American and South African History* (New York: Oxford University Press, 1981), xi.

[30] Robin DiAngelo, *White Fragility: Why It's So Hard for White People to Talk about Racism* (Boston: Beacon Press, 2018), 33.

would claim that Whiteness has biological and scientific foundations. Rather, today, most would regard Whiteness as socially
constructed. The social significance of Whiteness is guided not
by any biological or scientific foundations but by social meanings
attributed to it. When individuals refer to White people, either
in self-identification or a reference to a particular group, they are
generally referring to Whiteness—that is, a social construct "where
white cultural norms and practices go unnamed and unques-
tioned," but that has real and tangible effects.[31]

While Whiteness is an unmarked category for Whites, it is
quite visible to people of color. Moreover, Whiteness and White
people carry separate and nonresembling marks of distinction to
the degree that, as George Lipsitz puts it, "opposing whiteness is
not the same thing as opposing white people."[32]

Karen Teel, professor of theology and religious studies at
the University of San Diego, provides us with a caution that "as
a cultural identity, whiteness is not simply coextensive with all
racially white people; whites can try to opt out, and nonwhites can
try to opt in."[33] Nevertheless, White supremacy, in all manifestations, has contributed to the widespread disadvantages encountered
by people of color in American society. In 1989, women's studies
scholar Peggy McIntosh flipped the script to provide an alternative
argument to Whiteness as an unmarked category by interrogating
it from the perspective of the unearned advantages that White
people carry with them in everyday life.[34] She called this White

---

[31] Ruth Frankenberg, *The Social Construction of Whiteness: White Women,
Race Matters* (Minneapolis: University of Minnesota Press, 1993), 10.

[32] George Lipsitz, *The Possessive Investment in Whiteness: How White People
Profit from Identity Politics* (Philadelphia: Temple University Press, 1998), 8.

[33] Karen Teel, "Whiteness in Catholic Theological Method," *Journal
of the American Academy of Religion* 87, no. 2 (2019): 9.

[34] Melissa Stein, "Whiteness—African American Studies," *Oxford Bibli-*

privilege. Unlike Grant and Stoddard, who assumed the superiority of the White race, McIntosh, in her classic article, "White Privilege: Unpacking the Invisible Knapsack," focused on the unearned advantages or privileges that Whiteness conferred upon White people: "I realized I had been taught about racism as something that puts others at a disadvantage, but had been taught not to see one of its corollary aspects, White privilege, which puts me at an advantage."[35] McIntosh reflects on how she was implicated in perpetuating invisible systems of Whiteness: "I was taught to recognize racism only in individual acts of meanness by members of my group, never in invisible systems conferring unsought racial dominance on my group from birth."[36]

Other Terms and Their Uses
When We Talk about Race and Racism

A few final introductory words, before we begin.

In following the *Chicago Manual of Style*, the word "Black" will be capitalized throughout this book when referring to people of African descent. This is also in line with the capitalization of other racial and ethnic groups like Asian, Latinx, and Native. To keep it consistent, the word "White" will also be capitalized when referring to racial and ethnic identity. This includes concepts such as "Whiteness" and "White supremacy."

The term "Asian American" was coined by Yuji Ichioka, American historian and civil rights activist, in 1968 when he and Emma

---

ographies, February 27, 2019, https://www.oxfordbibliographies.com/view/document/obo-9780190280024/obo-9780190280024-0063.xml.

[35] Peggy McIntosh, "White Privilege: Unpacking the Invisible Knapsack," *Peace and Freedom* (1989):1, https://psychology.umbc.edu/files/2016/10/White-Privilege_McIntosh-1989.pdf.

[36] Ibid.

Gee founded the Asian American Political Alliance to unite Japanese, Chinese, and Filipino students at the University of California, Berkeley.[37] Asian American was originally conceived not simply as an umbrella term but as a political category of building solidarity across a wide variety of increasingly diverse ethnic groups from East Asia, South Asia (such as Desi), Southeast Asia, and other parts of Asia (such as Singaporean, Malaysian, and Indonesian).

While the label Asian American remains a political and essential category today, issues confronted by Asian Americans and Pacific Islanders are often ethnic group specific. Thus, henceforward this book will most often use "Asian" or a Pacific Islander ethnic-specific group (e.g., "Chinese American" or "Chamorro American"), rather than the umbrella term Asian American or AAPI to refer to Asian and Pacific Islander victims of hate crimes. While the USCCB use the collective political identity, Asian and Pacific Islanders, in their documents, the term, as Dawn Lee Tu points out, "does not reflect the experience of Pacific Islanders who have and continue to experience a unique set of struggles relating to sovereignty and decolonization, and do not fit into the model minority stereotype which paints Asian Americans as successful, assimilated into the American mainstream."[38]

And as this book examines the toxic stereotypes of the yellow peril, model minority, and perpetual foreigner, and many of these issues are more salient to Asian Americans than are the unique set of issues and struggles confronted by Pacific Islanders, I will focus mainly on Asian American experiences with an emphasis on Chinese American history. Discussion of the history and unique experiences of Pacific Islanders is beyond the scope of this volume.

---

[37] Caitlin Yoshiko Kandil, "After 50 Years of 'Asian American,' Advocates Say the Term Is 'More Essential than Ever,'" *NBC News,* May 31, 2018.
[38] Frances Kai-Hwa Wang, "Asian Americans and Pacific Islanders—a FAQ," *NBC News*, May 1, 2019.

Organization of This Volume

The book is divided into four chapters. This introductory chapter has provided a brief overview as well as an explanation of the style, terms, and concepts essential to a fruitful discussion of racism today. It has also provided critiques by various reviewers of the pastoral letter against racism, *Open Wide Our Hearts*, and my own critique of the pastoral response to Asian and Pacific Island Americans, *Encountering Christ in Harmony*.

The next three chapters investigate toxic stereotypes that shape the life and experiences of Asians in the United States, namely, the yellow peril, the model minority, and the perpetual foreigner. These three stereotypes are not mutually exclusive. They reinforce not only feelings of exclusion, marginalization, and a decreased sense of belonging in American society among Asian Americans but have also contributed to an upsurge of anti-Asian hate and violence during the recent pandemic.

Chapter 1 provides a historical examination of the portrayal of the Chinese and other Asians as yellow peril, the racialized stereotype that they are "disease-ridden," "unfair competitors," and that Asians are unassimilable and a threat to the White American way of life. This stereotype negatively impacted the lives of Chinese immigrants in the nineteenth century not only in their interimmigrant relationship with Americans of Irish descent but also in the public health arena. The chapter examines how Irish Catholics, who were persecuted for their Catholic faith when they first arrived in the United States, within a few decades became the oppressor by adopting the nativist racism of Anglo-Saxon Whites and persecuted the Chinese to better their position in the American racial hierarchy.

In public health crises, the yellow peril myth was routinely evoked by elected officials as well as by the federal government to justify hatred and mistreatment of Asian Americans. The moral virus of hate and racism has been a part of the United States even before the Chinese arrived in significant numbers in the mid-nineteenth century. In this way, COVID-19 has simply brought to the surface sinful deeds of our collective past that we had ignored and not adequately dealt with. This sort of moral evil, deeply embedded in the ideology of White supremacy, what James Cone[39] and Jim Wallis[40] have called "America's original sin," goes against what the US bishops' pastoral letter on racism discussed by emphasizing that the dignity of every human person is to be respected because we are created in the image and likeness of God.

Chapter 2 employs methodology from current Asian American studies to examine the model minority myth and the racial positioning of Asian Americans in the dynamic of the Black/White relationship. The difference in how Black and Asian Americans are racialized stems from the positions Black and Asian Americans are placed at in comparison to the dominant group. African Americans are placed in the bottom of the Black/White binary where they are seen as inferior to Whites, whereas Asian Americans are placed on an insider/outsider spectrum, where they are perceived as either perpetual foreigners, a model minority, or both at the same time. Claire Jean Kim clarifies that racial triangulation occurs when the dominant group pits Asian Americans against African Americans in particular on cultural and/or racial grounds. While Whites valorize Asian Americans relative to Blacks, the dominant group also constructs Asian Americans as immutably foreign and unassimilable to the American context. This portrayal as forever foreigners has left Asian Americans vulnerable to cycles of aggres-

---

[39] James H. Cone, "Theology's Great Sin: Silence in the Face of White Supremacy," in *Soul Work: Anti-Racist Theologies in Dialogue*, ed. Marjorie Bowers-Wheatley and Nancy Palmer Jones (Boston: Skinner House Books, 2003), 2.

[40] Jim Wallis, *America's Original Sin: Racism, White Privilege, and the Bridge to a New America* (Grand Rapids, MI: Brazos Press, 2016), 33–34.

sion from Whites but also from Blacks, Latinx, and other people of color. Here, distinction must be made between the individual violent crimes committed against Asian Americans from the deeper systemic racism embedded at institutional and structural levels. The chapter concludes by examining personal and corporate failures to "walk humbly with your God" (Mi 6:8) that goes against the grain of the long-standing emphasis of the biblical notion of justice put forth in the pastoral letter against racism.

Chapter 3 uses Jung Young Lee's theology of marginality to explore the perpetual foreigner stereotype, a permanent fixture in American society that has marked Asian Americans as unassimilable aliens and perpetual foreigners since the first wave of Asians stepped foot on American soil. The forever foreigner stereotype is how White supremacy operates through the model minority myth and is intimately linked with almost every anti-Asian xenophobia and violent crime committed against Asians and Asian Americans. This has been manifested in the current outbreaks of hate and violence against Asian Americans, bolstered by the insistence of former President Trump's reference to COVID-19 as the "Chinese virus" or "Kung Flu." The use of such ethnic slurs or racially charged terms has further shaped the perception of Asian Americans as forever foreigners. It does not matter how many generations Asians have been in the United States, or what positions of authority they hold, the perpetual foreigner stereotype prevents us from being embraced as true Americans. From the perspective of the Christian faith and Catholic Social Thought, more than just a sense of belonging to America is involved here. To repudiate the view of Asian Americans as foreigners is to recognize the inherent dignity of Asian Americans as persons in Christ.

The concluding chapter explores the biblical depiction of Jesus's experience of the three toxic stereotypes experienced by Asian Americans, followed by a theological reflection on the good news for the poor, and the magisterium's formulation of the preferential option for the poor. The chapter will conclude by looking at the various ways in which many elements of CST are already reflected in the practices of community-based organizations working with the marginalized in AAPI communities. While the encyclicals of the Catholic Church and pastoral letters of the USCCB do not directly address the social issues confronted by Asian Americans, the value of the CST principles is reflected in community-based interventions of Stop AAPI Hate, Asian Americans Advancing Justice–Los Angeles, Chinese for Affirmative Action, and other Asian American organizations that build bridges with the African American community and activist organizations. Together they establish allyship with other people of color, embracing a restorative justice model in resolving racial and ethnic conflicts, and promote social justice and peace.

1

Yellow Peril

In his executive action, signed on January 26, 2021, to combat the skyrocketing of xenophobia and racism against the Asian American Pacific Islander community, President Joe Biden underscored that anti-Asian racism is "unacceptable" and "un-American." It is indeed unacceptable to treat another group of human beings with hate and dehumanizing behavior which, unfortunately, has deep roots in the American tradition.

The Othering of immigrants or foreigners with infectious disease and concomitant cruel treatment is something that has been repeated throughout US history. In 1793, Germans were alleged to have brought yellow fever or the "German flu" into the country. In 1832 and 1849, the Irish were blamed for cholera epidemics in New York City. From 1870 to 1905, the Chinese were to become medical scapegoats by health officials in Hawaii and those on the West Coast for their failure to contain smallpox, bubonic plague, and other epidemic outbreaks.[1] In 1916, Italians were suspected of polio outbreaks, whereas tuberculosis was associated with the Jewish population.[2] But while Germans, Irish, and other European immigrants were eventually folded into the wider racial category of

---

[1] Joan B. Trauner, "The Chinese as Medical Scapegoats in San Francisco, 1870–1905," *Chinese in California* 57, no. 1 (Spring 1978): 70.

[2] Erika Lee, "Americans Are Dangerous, Disease-Carrying Foreigners Now," *Washington Post*, July 8, 2020.

Whiteness, given legal privileges and access to property ownership and civil rights, no longer seen as carriers of diseases, the Chinese and other Asians, due to our physical visibility and supposedly "alien" cultural differences, were depicted as yellow peril.

This vicious term is a racial construct that emerged in Europe during the nineteenth century in response to the fear of an invasion of uncivilized, low-intelligence, and dangerous people from Asia, Chinese in particular, who posed a serious threat to the presumably more civilized White nations of the West.[3] In the United States, yellow peril was a racialized stereotype of unassimilable aliens who were susceptible to contagions and posed biomedical and growing economic threats to White workers in the nineteenth century.

In the early twentieth century, the most recognizable, fictional yellow peril character was Dr. Fu Manchu, the diabolical mastermind introduced by British author Sax Rohmer and featured extensively in radio, television, cinema, and comic strips for many decades. During the Second World War, Fu Manchu embodied yellow peril, the growing sense of geopolitical menace felt by many Americans because of the growing military might of Japan. Fu Manchu reinforced the worst of the perverted stereotypes of Asian Americans and left an indelible mark on the collective American memory.[4]

Today, the racialized stereotype of Asians and Asian Americans continues on as the viral threat, reemerging during the COVID-19 pandemic. While the perpetual foreigner stereotype is always present in the life of Asian American and Pacific Islanders (AAPI), the yellow peril stereotype engenders fear that leads to the rise in hate and violence against AAPI.

---

[3] David White, "The Theory of Yellow Peril," Study.com, July 9, 2021, https://study.com/academy/lesson/the-theory-of-yellow-peril.html.

[4] Joseph Cheah and Grace Ji-Sun Kim, *Theological Reflection on "Gangnam Style": A Racial, Sexual, and Cultural Critique* (New York: Palgrave Macmillan, 2014), 16–17.

Even before March 11, 2020, the date when the World Health Organization declared COVID-19 a pandemic, Asian American academics, activists, and community organizers sounded the alarm that the outbreak of the virus in China could lead to a rise in anti-Asian hate and violence in the United States. This is confirmed by the arrival of "Stop AAPI Hate," a reporting center established by the Asian Pacific Planning and Policy Council (A3PCON), Chinese for Affirmative Action, and the Asian American Studies Department of San Francisco State University for the purpose of collecting, tracking, and responding to incidents of hate, violence, harassment, discrimination, shunning, and child bullying against AAPI.[5] The center received 1,497 incident reports within two weeks after it was launched on March 19, 2020. It has identified hate incidents as verbal harassment, shunning, coughing at or spitting upon, violent physical assault, and barring from an establishment and transportation. Barring from an establishment and transportation constitutes civil rights violations. Physical assault, as well as coughing at and spitting upon another person, which pose public health concerns, can be classified as either a hate incident or a hate crime. From March 19, 2020, to December 31, 2021, Stop AAPI Hate reported a total of 10,905 hate incidents against AAPI persons, of which women accounted for 61.8 percent of hate violence, a rate almost 2.3 times higher than that of their male counterparts. Nationally, one in five Asian Americans (21.2 percent) and Pacific Islanders (20 percent) experienced hate incidents during this period. Physical assaults constituted 16.1 percent of all complaints, and businesses were the primary site of discrimination. In terms of ethnic groups, Chinese reported "the most hate incidents (42.8%), followed by Korean (16.1%), P/Filinpx (8.9%),

---

[5] "Asian American & Pacific Islander Historical Timeline," *Stop AAPI Hate*, https://stopaapihate.org/timeline/.

Japanese (8.2%), and Vietnamese (8%)."[6] Among AAPI youth, a quarter experienced racist bullying, not simply verbal harassment but also physical attacks. These are the figures for people who submitted an incident report to Stop AAPI Hate. Because many in the Asian American immigrant community do not report hate incidents to authorities for various reasons, including language and culture, the actual number of incidents is surely much higher.

Yellow Peril in the Nineteenth Century

Even before the Chinese arrived in significant numbers in the mid-nineteenth century, many Americans regarded China as a country in serious decline and its citizens as "nothing more than starving masses, beasts of burden, depraved heathens, and opium addicts."[7] By the 1850s, the Chinese arrived in notable numbers to search for gold in California. It did not take long for White miners to demand that they be protected from foreign miners, Chinese in particular. The nativist outcry was devious because the Chinese could only work on claims already abandoned by White miners. In May 1852, after the recommendation of a committee to the California Assembly, the new California Governor John Bigler passed the foreign miners' license tax, which required every foreign miner who did not wish to become an American citizen to pay three dollars per month. This was increased to four dollars in 1853, six dollars in 1855, and a two-dollar increase each year thereafter.[8] The foreign miners' tax was directed at the Chinese who, even if they so desired, could not have

---

[6] "Stop AAPI Hate National Report," *Stop AAPI Hate*, https://stopaapihate. org/wp-content/uploads/2022/03/22-SAH-NationalReport-3.2.22-v9.pdf.

[7] Sucheng Chan, "Hostility and Conflict," in *Asian American Studies,* ed. Jean Yu-wen Shen Wu and Min Song (New Brunswick, NJ: Rutgers University Press, 2000), 48.

[8] Jean Pfaelzer, *Driven Out: The Forgotten War against Chinese Americans* (Berkeley: University of California Press, 2007), 31.

become citizens as the 1790 Naturalization Act reserved naturalized citizenship to only free White people.[9] This was the first instance in which the Chinese were legally marked as non-Americans or foreigners, a characterization that feeds into the yellow peril trope.

In the 1860s, there was an expansion of labor-intensive industries, and the greatest demand for Chinese laborers was in heavy construction work on the Central Pacific Railroad. Unable to find a sufficient number of White workers to lay railroad tracks east of Sacramento, Chinese migrants were recruited to take on the dangerous and backbreaking work in building the western portion of the transcontinental railway that runs through the granite mountains of the Sierra Nevada. These workers demonstrated heroic efforts in laying the harshest section of railroad tracks by boring tunnels through the granite rocks of the Sierra spires and laying tracks across the deserts of Nevada and Utah. The Central Pacific Railroad employed more than 12,000 Chinese laborers at the peak of construction in 1868 and, by the time it was completed a year later, more than 1,200 Chinese had lost their lives.

The completion of the transcontinental railroad on May 10, 1869, was marked by the driving of the golden spike at Promontory Point, Utah. There were 1,500 people present at this ceremony, including politicians and other prominent individuals from across the country, railroad workers from the Central Pacific and Union Pacific Railroads, five companies of soldiers from the twenty-first US infantry regiment, and members of the public. The most famous photo associated with the Golden Spike Ceremony is Andrew J. Russell's "East and West Shaking Hands at Laying of Last Rail," commonly known as "The Champagne Photo."[10] It captured the meeting of two trains at Promontory Point with many jubilant men

---

[9] Ronald Takaki, *Strangers from a Different Shore* (Boston: Back Bay Books, 1998), 82.

[10] "Andrew J. Russell: The Champagne Photo," *National Park Service*, nps.gov.

in front of and on top of the engines. What is striking about this iconic photo is the absence of Chinese laborers who constructed the line with the sweat of their brow and at a great cost. This was another instance of the forever foreigner trope in which Chinese were seen as non-Americans or foreigners, and their contributions were not fully acknowledged and erased from history.

In *Minor Feelings: An Asian American Reckoning*, Cathy Park Hong, a poet, cultural critic, and professor, states, "Three Chinese laborers died for every two miles of track built to make Manifest Destiny a reality, but when the celebratory photo of the Golden Spike was taken, not a single Chinese man was welcome to pose with the other—white—railroad workers."[11] The deliberate omission of the Chinese in Russell's photograph serves as a metaphor of how often Chinese or AAPI have been tokenized, misrepresented, omitted, or rendered invisible.

After 1869, the year of the completion of the transcontinental railroad, many Chinese laborers toiled in low-paying manufacturing jobs in the cigar, shoe, and garment industries, or entered physical labor jobs, becoming farmers, gardeners, cooks, and laundry workers. Many who settled in Chinatowns on the West Coast—about 24 percent of California's Chinese population resided in San Francisco[12]—were adherents to a syncretistic religion comprising Buddhism, Confucianism, and Daoism. Their religious expressions were deemed alien, which fed into yellow peril fears and further enflamed anti-Chinese sentiments. They established temples, often mocked as "joss houses," which anti-Chinese vigilante groups took pleasure in burning down. Indeed, the "strangeness" of their culture, assumed unassimilability of their way of life, and so-called superstitious elements embedded in their

---

[11] Cathy Park Hong, *Minor Feelings: An Asian American Reckoning* (New York: One World, 2020), 20.

[12] Takaki, *Strangers from a Different Shore,* 79.

"heathen" religion were some of the rationales used by Senator A. A. Sargent when he argued before the US Senate in 1878 to prohibit further immigration from China to the United States. Sargent criticized the religious beliefs and practices of Chinese immigrants as an expression of a pagan religion, which hindered them from assimilating into a White Christian nation. Instead of converting the Chinese in the United States, as proposed by some Protestant clerics, Sargent advocated banning immigration until such a time that Christian missionaries could travel to China and convert the Chinese to the Christian faith.[13] This illustrates the idea that becoming Christian makes Chinese people Whiter.

Chinese customs and religious expressions were so different that the Chinese could never become part of American society until they were made Whiter by converting them to White Christianity. This exemplifies how the concepts of Whiteness and Christianity have been bound together since the formation of the United States. Religion and culture were deeply intertwined, and concepts of Whiteness and Christianity were bound together to reflect the association of Whiteness with Christianity and being American.[14]

Those who came to the United States were mainly young Chinese men, and those who were married were not allowed to bring their wives because Americans wanted the Chinese labor but not Chinese families. Early Chinatowns, where many of them were forced to live, reflected common vices of a bachelor society, which included a thriving vice economy based on gambling, prostitution, and drugs. So it did not bode well for Chinese migrants when the "yellow journalism" of sensational print media portrayed Chinatowns as breeding grounds for disease, depravity, and degradation, which found widespread acceptance with the American populace.

[13] Cited in Jeannine Hill Fletcher, *The Sin of White Supremacy: Christianity, Racism, and White Supremacy in America* (Maryknoll, NY: Orbis Books, 2017), 1.

[14] Ibid.

As the Chinese population grew in California, so did xeno-phobia and racism directed toward them. They were racialized and dehumanized as "dog eaters" and associated with vermin like rats and mice. During the outbreak of smallpox in 1875–76, San Francisco officials blamed the Chinese in Chinatown for unsani-tary living conditions that endangered public health. This was also the case when the bubonic plague struck in 1900. The US surgeon general at the time labeled it an "Oriental disease, peculiar to rice eaters."[15] After a Chinese man died of the plague, city officials quar-antined twenty-five to thirty thousand Chinese residents in San Francisco Chinatown, while escorting White residents out. In both cases, the government officials targeted not only Chinatown but the Chinese body as the source of disease and contamination that posed a threat to public health.

When the bubonic plague broke out in Honolulu in 1900, the Territory of Hawai'i's 'Board of Health declared a state of emergency and set fire to forty-one buildings in Honolulu's China-town. A couple weeks later, another controlled fire was ignited in a "contaminated" area, but the wind gusts carried fire throughout the city. After that fire was contained in seventeen days, it had destroyed thirty-eight acres and four thousand homes of mostly Chinese and Japanese residents.[16]

In 1906, the Santa Ana city council in California justified setting the entire Chinatown on fire because a man found shan-ties there that allegedly had housed people with leprosy. Over a thousand local residents lined up to watch the fire while the local fire department stood by to protect the buildings surrounding

---

[15] F. M. Todd, *Eradicating Plague from San Francisco* (San Francisco: C. A. Murdock & Co., 1909), cited in Amanuel Elias, Jehonathan Ben, Fethi Mansouri, and Yin Paradies, "Racism and Nationalism during and beyond the COVID-19 Pandemic," *Ethnic and Racial Studies* 44, no. 5 (2021): 787.

[16] "Chinatown Fire of 1900," *Hawaii History.org*, http://www.hawaiihistory. org/index.cfm?fuseaction=ig.page&PageID=548.

Chinatown.[17] As xenophobic propaganda depicting the Chinese as "diseased bodies," "pathogenic carriers," and unassimilable to the American way of life spread throughout the country, they became an easy scapegoat for widespread violence and unnecessary destruction imposed onto them.

Irish and Chinese Immigrants

The Irish and the Chinese had similar immigration characteristics in that they came to the United States at a similar time, and both were persecuted for their race and religion. As the number of Irish Catholics increased substantially, they were soon seen as a threat to destroy the values and ethos of White Protestant America.[18] Similarly, when Chinese migrants arrived to search for gold and, later in the 1860s, served as contract or indentured workers to build the transcontinental railroad, they brought their syncretistic religion and settled mainly in California and elsewhere on the West Coast. They were forcibly separated into racial and ethnic enclaves popularly referred to as Chinatowns because racial segregation was the norm. Their religious difference also contributed to this racialized separation.

The Irish and Chinese began to flee to the United States starting in the 1840s and 1850s, respectively, to escape from economic chaos, political turmoil, and famine taking place in their native countries. Many Chinese immigrants considered themselves sojourners, working hard in the host society, sending remittances back home to support their poor families with the hope of earning enough money to return to China to assume a higher social status as a reward for their hard work in the United States.[19] For the

---

[17] Andrew R. Chow, "Violence against Asian Americans Is on the Rise: But It's Part of a Long History," *TIME*, May 20, 2020.

[18] Erika Lee, *America for Americans: A History of Xenophobia in the United States* (New York: Basic Books, 2019), 47.

[19] Yuen Fong-Woon, "The Voluntary Sojourners among Overseas

Irish, mass starvation caused by a fungus, *phytophthora infestans*, or "potato blight," which wiped out almost the entire potato crop in Ireland, caused over a million and a half to immigrate in the 1840s; by the following decade, they constituted 35 percent of all new immigrants. By 1860, one-quarter of New Yorkers were Irish, and the Irish immigrants outnumbered Anglo-Saxon Protestant Whites in Boston.

Fleeing from starvation and disease from famine-ridden Ireland, Irish immigrants were among the most impoverished to seek refuge in the United States. Most had no skills and were forced into the hardest and lowest-paying jobs. Because they often worked alongside African Americans, the widespread belief was that the Irish were simply "niggers turned inside out" and that African Americans were "smoked Irish." While in some scientific illustrations of the day, the Irish were depicted as ranking just a level or two above the animal kingdom, and described in some cartoons as having features of Black Americans, courts nevertheless endorsed the Whiteness of the Irish and other European immigrants. Some challenges and doubts about the Whiteness of the Celtic race notwithstanding, courts almost always treated those from Europe as legally White.[20] And, as mentioned above, the option of becoming a US citizen was available to Irish, Italians, and other European immigrants because the Naturalization Act of 1790 specified that only a free White person could apply for citizenship. Chinese, on the other hand, were considered heathens and treated as a "race problem," denied the right to become naturalized citizens.[21]

After the US Civil War (1861–65), many Irish immigrant laborers flooded into the state of California with the hope that they would find a new beginning in the West. During the period

---

Chinese: Myth or Reality?" *Public Affairs* 56, no. 4 (Winter 1983–84): 674.

[20] Philip Q. Yang and Kavitha Koshy, "The 'Becoming White Thesis' Revisited," *Journal of Public and Professional Sociology*, 8, no. 1 (March 2016): 9.

[21] Lee, *America for Americans*, 57–59, 81.

of economic depression that followed (1873–79), competition for jobs between Chinese and Irish laborers became increasingly acrimonious as the two marginal groups struggled for survival. Faced with economic downturn and labor market uncertainty, White workers blamed Chinese workers for competing unfairly and taking jobs from them, even though venture capitalists in the mining, railroad, and manufacturing industry recruited the Chinese, who worked longer hours and for less, using them to keep wages down and as pawns to break the demands of White labor unions.

The Chinese were blamed for working for lower wages and bringing down the standard of living of White Americans. In reality, their willingness to take low-paying jobs contributed to higher wages and living standards for Whites. Xenophobic racism of unemployed White workers reared its ugly head as it turned into violent racist attacks against Chinese laborers who were seen as threatening, unassimilable aliens who brought economic competition, disease, and depravity. Yellow peril discourses, which portrayed Chinese workers as unfair competitors, on the one hand, and disease carriers, on the other, were reinforced by racist cartoons, magazines, and political rhetoric resulting in lynchings, massacres, and mob violence against the Chinese. They were rounded up and systematically driven out of Portland, Seattle, and other cities on the West Voast.[22] In 1885 alone, the Chinese were expelled from Eureka, California; Tacoma, Washington; and massacred in Rock Springs, Wyoming. In February 1885, the entire Chinese population of Eureka was rounded up and driven off when David C. Kendall, a city councilman, was killed in a crossfire between two bickering Chinese men. The incident played into the hands of those who had been demanding, "The Chinese Must Go," a slogan popularized by an Irishman Kearney, whom I will discuss below. Within two days,

---

[22] Erika Lee, *The Making of Asian America: A History* (New York: Simon and Schuster, 2015), 93.

Eureka's humming Chinatown ceased to exist as approximately 480 Chinese were driven off to San Francisco.[23]

In September 1885, a labor dispute between White and Chinese coal miners turned into a carnage known as the "Rock Springs Massacre," leaving twenty-eight Chinese coal miners dead, fifteen wounded, and several hundred more driven out of town. In November 1885, an armed mob of approximately five hundred White citizens of Tacoma, Washington, forcibly drove an entire Chinese population of about six hundred out of Tacoma to Portland, Oregon. The precipitating event was the action of the water company who hired Chinese instead of White workers to lay pipe in the city.[24] These are just three examples of more than 150 anti-Asian riots and expulsions of the Chinese that swept through the American West between 1885 and 1887 alone.

Religion, Race, and Chinese Exclusion

Because Irish Catholics were the most vociferous in their opposition to the Chinese, priests who ministered to them were often outspoken critics of the Chinese as well. This was the case with Father James Chrysostom Bouchard, a Jesuit priest and popular Roman Catholic orator who, on February 25, 1873, gave a speech before a packed audience in St. Francis of Assisi Church in San Francisco as a fundraiser for the Presentation Sisters. In his speech concerning the question "White Man or Chinaman—Which?" Bouchard advocated limiting immigration to European immigrants: "'Tis the white race we want. . . . They come from the islands and from the continent of Europe; are bone of our bone—our own kind."[25] Bouchard endorsed

---

[23] Lynwood Carranco, "Chinese Expulsion from Humboldt County," *Pacific Historical Review* 30, no. 4 (November 1961): 329.

[24] Jules Alexander Karlin, "The Anti-Chinese Outbreak in Tacoma, 1885," *Pacific Historical Review* 23, no. 3 (August 1954): 272.

[25] Jeffrey Burns et al., *Keeping Faith: European and Asian Catholic Immigrants* (Maryknoll, NY: Orbis Books, 2000), 233–34.

a White supremacist way of thinking that sought to make America a White person's country. He passionately opposed immigration of the Chinese, whom he considered to be "ignorant idolators," an inferior race, pagans, and immoral creatures "incapable of rising to the virtue that is inculcated by the religion of Jesus Christ."[26]

Bouchard demonized the Chinese as a way of limiting the Catholic Church's membership to those of European descent. Paradoxically, what he kept hidden from his audience was his own racial/ethnic background: Bouchard was a Native American of the Delaware tribe. His mother was of French descent and had been adopted by Comanches as a girl. Had his audience known this, the reception to his speech might have been different, given prevailing stereotypes about the savagery of Indians in nineteenth-century California. Nonetheless, Bouchard's background illustrates how Christianity and Whiteness were bound together to the degree that Bouchard found acceptance among Whites through his conversion to Christianity, especially as a member of the sacerdotal class. In other words, Bouchard benefited from the Christian missionary effort in his native tribe, yet condemned the same kind of missionary work extended to the Chinese.[27]

In 1870, San Francisco's population was composed of over 40 percent foreign-born Europeans, with Irish Catholics representing the largest group. In a society that emphasized Whiteness and English-speaking citizens, the Irish began to dominate the social and political life with a number of Irish Catholics, such as David Broderick and John Downey, elected to state government. As a result, many Protestant leaders in San Francisco began issuing warnings about the perilous threat Catholics posed. Old racial and religious prejudices that the Irish experienced in the eastern colonies and states were reinscribed on the West Coast as

---

[26] Burns et al., *Keeping Faith*, 234.
[27] Joshua Paddison, "Anti-Catholicism and Race in Post-Civil War San Francisco," *Pacific Historical Review* 78, no. 4 (2009): 506.

San Francisco's Irish Catholics were soon seen as less than White and Christian.

To counter such prejudice, Irish Catholics began scape-goating Chinese as racial and religious Others. The rise of the anti-Chinese movement in the early 1880s and the construction of the Chinese as a "common danger" for both Irish Catholics and older White Protestant groups, provided Irish Catholics with the perfect opportunity to put themselves on the side of White Christian patriotism by Othering the Chinese.[28] By the late nineteenth century, White Protestants and Catholics had united around the idea of White Christianity serving as the basis of a definition of American identity.[29]

One notorious proponent of anti-Chinese exclusion and agitator for the White working class during the depression of the 1870s was the immigrant Irishman named Denis Kearney, mentioned above. Known as "the people's dictator," Kearney exploited economic insecurity in the working class by delivering scathing speeches, denouncing business capitalists, and the presence of Chinese in California. In 1877, Kearney, as a representative of Draymen and Teamsters, launched the Workingmen's Party of California to advocate for fair wages for White workers and to "rid the country of cheap Chinese labor."[30] Kearney despised the

---

[28] Ibid., 510, 519.

[29] In the South, the rise and acceptance of Jim Crow was in part due to northern and southern Protestants uniting around the same idea of White Christianity as a basis for defining American identity. In other words, there was a historical process by which even Protestants turned against people of color in order to embrace Whiteness. See Edward J. Blum, *Reforging the White Republic: Race, Religion, and American Nationalism, 1865–1898* (Baton Rouge, LA: LSU Press, 2005); Grant R. Brodrecht, *Our Country: Northern Evangelicals and the Union during the Civil War Era* (New York: Fordham University Press, 2018).

[30] Theodore J. O'Keefe, "Denis Kearney & the Struggle for a White America," Counter-Currents.com, February 1, 2011.

Chinese and resorted to popular racist sentiments to justify the exclusion of Chinese immigrants. He peppered his incendiary speeches with anti-Chinese invectives of the day (e.g., "leprous, rat-eating Chinese slaves") and ended speeches with the cry, "The Chinese must go!"[31]

In October 1877, Kearney spoke outside San Francisco's Nob Hill, where such wealthy landowners as Charles Crooker, Leland Stanford, and Mark Hopkins resided, and told workers to arm themselves, for the "dignity of labor must be sustained, even if we have to kill every wretch that opposes it."[32] Such inflammatory speeches made a lot of people, including church officials, uncomfortable. While these officials and even capitalists agreed on the restrictions of Chinese immigration, they opposed the violent language and revolting epithets employed by Kearney.

When denouncing Kearney's Workingmen's Party's inflammatory rhetoric and the violence he was advocating against the Chinese, Archbishop Joseph Sadoc Alemany of San Francisco[33] and other Catholic leaders made it clear that they too opposed the influx of "Chinese incubus," but the correct way to restrict such immigration was to do it "quietly, legally, and constitutionally" through lawful redress that came from the government.[34] Though a cradle Catholic, Kearney's relationship to the Church was adversarial, and he openly censured Archbishop Alemany for interfering in "temporal affairs." Kearney's stubborn persistence in his agita-

---

[31] Kevin Jenks, "Denis Kearney and the Chinese Exclusion Acts," *Straight Thinking on Immigration* 6, no. 3 (1996).

[32] William Doherty, "The Prole and the Prelate," MUShare. December 5, 2017, https://mushare.marian.edu/concern/generic_works/9d198c41-5711-49f2-85e4-e74813179c54.

[33] Archbishop Joseph S. Alemany dedicated the Old Saint Mary's of the Immaculate Conception as the first cathedral of the Archdiocese of San Francisco in 1854.

[34] Josh Paddison, *American Heathens: Religion, Race, and Reconstruction in California* (Berkeley: University of California Press, 2012), 126.

tion, which threatened social peace, prompted Alemany to issue three pastoral letters, urging Catholics to "stand by authority" and to prohibit them from participation at rallies that were "seditious, antisocial, and anti-Christian meetings."[35]

Archbishop Alemany was against violent means of opposing the influx of Chinese in California for fear that it would feed into anti-Catholic hysteria, as Irish Catholics were considered by Anglo-Saxon Protestants as neither fully White nor fully Christian. And Alemany's displeasure and opposition to Kearney's confrontational approach did much to dissolve the cohesiveness of his Workingmen's Party of California (WPC).[36] The decline of the WPC freed California's Catholic leadership to openly denounce Chinese immigration without the danger of being associated with Kearney's militant radicalism. While Archbishop Alemany showed care and concern toward Chinese immigrants within his diocese, he also bolstered Irish Catholics' claims to Whiteness and desire to identify as White patriotic Christians when he signed his name to the 1879 public petition to restrict Chinese immigration.[37] In so doing, Catholics added their voices to the formation and consolidation of White Christian nationalism.

That same year, James Gilmary Shea, a "liberal" Irish American historian, wrote in *American Catholic Quarterly Review* that although crime and vice could be found in the Irish community, the Irishman, by nature, was "pure, virtuous, healthy in body and in morals" and "the fact remains that the Chinese element intro-

---

[35] John B. McGloin, *California's First Archbishop: The Life of Joseph Sadoc Alemany, O.P., 1814–1888* (New York: Herder and Herder, 1966), 294–95.

[36] "Holy Cross Cemetery/Archbishop Joseph Sadoc Alemany, O.P.," *National Park Service*, November 17, 2004, https://www.nps.gov/parkhistory/online_books/5views/5views5h41.htm.

[37] Paddison, "Anti-Catholicism and Race in Post-Civil War San Francisco," 534.

duces new forms of vice."[38] Like many other Irish Catholics, Shea
was a strong advocate for the exclusion of the Chinese. Though
definitely in the minority, there were among the Irish laity those
who were pro-Chinese immigration. One of them was Patrick J.
Healy, an Irish-born shoemaker and law student who offered his
unusual testimony at a second hearing on Chinese immigration
in San Francisco in 1879. He thought paganism was just as moral
a religion as Christianity and was not opposed to intermarriages
between the "Irish and Mongolians."[39]

The WPC movement was short-lived, but Kearney's WPC
managed to rewrite anti-Chinese codes into the second California
constitution. This stipulated that the presence of foreigners who
were ineligible for citizenship was dangerous to the well-being
of the state and that no state, county, municipality, or corpora-
tion could employ the Chinese.[40] In addition, Kearney's agitation
helped awaken American workers across the nation to alleged problems posed by Chinese workers, even though the real problem was
not the Chinese but the capitalists who exploited them as strike
breakers and as workers willing to labor for low wages. Nevertheless, the antipathy of many White workers against the Chinese
encouraged politicians of all stripes to court large anti-Chinese,
working-class votes, which eventually contributed to the movement to restrict Chinese immigration.

The debate in Congress over the Chinese Exclusion Bill was
filled with anti-Chinese rhetoric. At a congressional meeting on
February 28, 1882, Senator John F. Miller of California introduced
this legislation to exclude Chinese immigrant laborers from the
United States. In his argument, he employed the yellow peril image

---

[38] James Gilmary Shea, *American Catholic Quarterly Review*, vol. 4 (Philadelphia: Hardy & Mahony, January–October 1879), 249, 353.

[39] Paddison, "Anti-Catholicism and Race in Post-Civil War San Francisco," 537–38.

[40] Pfaelzer, *Driven Out*, 79.

of untold millions of the "degraded and inferior race" invading American shores and, therefore, becoming a threat to national security. Only a few members of Congress opposed the bill. Massachusetts Senator George Frisbie Hoar called it discriminatory, an "old race prejudice" that went against the ideal of the Declaration of Independence.[41] Blanche K. Bruce, the lone African American Senator from Mississippi, voted against the racist legislation. His comment was expounded in the *Christian Recorder*, an African American newspaper in Boston: "Only a few years ago, the cry was, not 'The Chinese must go' but 'The niggers must go' and it came from the same strata of society. There is not a man to-day who rails out against the yellow man from China but would equally rail out against the black man if opportunity only afforded."[42]

In the end, the writing was on the wall that the bill would pass with little opposition. Of the 325 seats in the US House of Representatives, only thirty-seven opposed the bill.[43] On May 6, 1882, when President Chester A. Arthur signed it into law, the Catholic hierarchy was silent in that they neither lobbied Congress against Chinese Exclusion, like some Republican Protestant clergy did, nor did they issue public statements denouncing this racist act.

To be sure, the US Catholic Church in the late nineteenth century was an immigrant and persecuted church. The founding of the National Catholic War Council, the forerunner of the National Catholic Welfare Conference, which has been known since 2001 as the United States Conference of Catholic Bishops (USCCB), was still over three decades away. Because there was no national bishops' organization until 1917, lobbying Congress to oppose the Chinese Exclusion Act would have had to be done by individual

---

[41] Lee, *America for Americans*, 92.

[42] Cited in Gary Y. Okihiro, *Margins and Mainstreams: Asians in American History and Culture* (Seattle: University of Washington Press, 1994), 48.

[43] Cited in Diana L. Eck, *Encountering God: A Spiritual Journey from Bozeman to Banaras* (Boston: Beacon Press, 1993), 34.

bishops. Unfortunately, there was no prophetic voice among the
bishops of John England's caliber, a native of Ireland, who vehe-
mently supported Jewish emancipation in this country during his
tenure as the first Roman Catholic bishop of Charleston, South
Carolina.[44] Even Archbishop Alemany, who showed concerns for
the Chinese in his diocese by sponsoring a Chinese priest, Father
Thomas Cian of the Congregation of Holy Family to work with
them, still signed a petition to restrict Chinese immigration.[45]
During the forty-year period between the death of Bishop England
in 1842 and the passage of the Chinese Exclusion Act in 1882, it
appears that no Catholic bishop took an openly critical stance to
oppose the Chinese exclusion prior to the enactment of the act—
either to endorse the many Catholics who were in opposition to
the act or to condemn those who advocated its passage.

By remaining silent to the sinful actions of many Irish Catholics who adopted nativist ideology and practices toward the
Chinese by persecuting them at every turn, and who actively advocated for their exclusion from immigrating to the United States,
the Catholic Church was guilty of the sin of omission as noted in
the bishops' 2018 pastoral letter: "[T]oo often racism comes in the
form of the sin of omission, when individuals, communities, and
even churches remain silent and fail to act against racial injustice
when it is encountered."[46] Religion and race, undoubtedly, played a
role in the silence of the leadership. Had Congress considered the
exclusion of the Irish, rather than the Chinese, I have no doubt the

---

[44] Leo D. Lefebure, *Transforming Interreligious Relations: Catholic
Responses to Religious Pluralism in the United States* (Maryknoll, NY: Orbis
Books, 2020), 107.

[45] Burns et al., *Keeping Faith*, 234. Father Cian did not work out as he
spoke a different dialect and could not communicate with the Chinese in San
Francisco who came from the Cantonese-speaking province of Guandong.

[46] US Conference of Catholic Bishops, *Open Wide Our Hearts: The
Enduring Call to Love—A Pastoral Letter Against Racism* (Washington, DC:
USCCB, 2018), 2.

Catholic bishops and priests would have spoken up. That would have been the right thing to do for the Irish. It was also the right thing to do for the so-called "heathen" Chinese and foreign Others. Acknowledgment of the complicity of the Church is essential for the formation of an antiracist institution.

In contrast, there was a minority of vocal Protestant clerics who not only staunchly condemned the unchristian behavior of Kearney but, more importantly, threw themselves boldly into the struggle against national legislation designed to prevent Chinese workers from entering the United States. Protestant clergy looked upon the presence of the Chinese on American shores as an opportunity provided by God to convert them to the Christian faith; the converted might then help spread Christianity to their countrymen and women when they returned to China. Protestant missionary supporters of Chinese immigration thought that Chinese immigrants who found themselves in an alien culture and thousands of miles away from their families, friends, and religious support might be primed for conversion to Christianity. The hope was that they might become even more disengaged from their own religious moorings as they left the city to labor on the railroad.

Presbyterian missionary Reverend William Speer felt that the Chinese might even forsake their own traditions as they worked on the railroad, considered to be the most leading-edge technology of the nineteenth century.[47] Presbyterians began this work of evangelizing the Chinese in 1853 under the direction of Reverend Speer, who stood out as the first champion of the persecuted Chinese. He viewed the spiritual and political needs of his Chinese parishioners as inseparable and "urged the legislature to support Chinese

---

[47] Kathryn Gin Lum, "Religion on the Road: How Chinese Migrants Adapted Popular Religion to an American Context," in *The Chinese and the Iron Road: Building the Transcontinental Railroad*, ed. Gordon H. Chang and Shelley Fisher Fishkin (Stanford, CA: Stanford University Press, 2019), 168–69.

immigration, lower the foreign miner's tax targeting the Chinese, protect their civil liberties, and allow them full testimony rights."[48] He established the first Christian church for Chinese immigrants in San Francisco in 1853, which was followed by Baptists in 1854, Episcopalians in 1855, Methodists in 1868, and Congregationalists in 1870.[49]

The arrival of Chinese workers in greater numbers—5,167 in 1868, 12,874 in 1869, and 15,730 in 1870[50]—spurred a fear of the yellow peril among the Whites of California, who saw it as an invasion of unassimilable heathens with a strange culture and "immoral habits." Protestant clergy defended Chinese newcomers as upright and polite people and assured doubters that whatever moral weaknesses they might possess would disappear once they received the Christian message. They knew that conversion to the Christian faith was central to the formation of race and citizenship in the postbellum United States.[51] This is how, by the 1870s, Protestant clergy and California businessmen became the main spokesmen for the Chinese, while Irish Catholics and the labor unions were among their principal opponents.[52]

Not all Protestant clergy were pro-Chinese, however. Baptist minister Isaac S. Kalloch, for instance, was known for his fiery anti-Chinese sermons and insisted that the evangelization of the Chinese should occur in China, not in California. He gave Kearney's movement legitimacy and a meeting place at his church, the Metropolitan Temple which, at the time, was the largest Baptist

---

[48] Paddison, *American Heathens*, 28.

[49] Robert Seager, "Some Denominational Reactions to Chinese Immigration to California, 1856–1892," *Pacific Historical Review* 28, no. 1 (1959): 49–66.

[50] United States Census Office, *Compendium of the Tenth Census (June 1, 1880): Compiled Pursuant to an Act of Congress Approved August 7, 1882* (Washington, DC: GPO, 1883), 380–84.

[51] Paddison, *American Heathens*, 4.

[52] Seager, "Some Denominational Reactions," 53–54.

church in the country. As the semiofficial chaplain of the WPC, Kalloch escalated his attacks against the Chinese, "renouncing the notion that they could ever be converted to Christianity under any circumstances."[53]

But Protestant clergy, on the whole, remained pro-Chinese under the leadership of Reverend Otis Gibson in the 1870s. Gibson was a missionary in Fuzhou, China, for ten years before he took charge of the Methodist missionary work among the Chinese immigrants on the West Coast of the United States. His book, *The Chinese in America,* provided a pro-Chinese ecclesiastical perspective and was utilized by legislators and clergy. Also, Reverend Gibson had no love for the Catholic Church. This is reflected not only in Protestants' reaction to the First Vatican Council (1869–70), in which the dogma of infallibility was defined,[54] but also in the era's sectarian battles that pitted Catholics against Protestants in debates over schooling, voting, and political influences. So, when Reverend James Bouchard, a prominent Jesuit priest, asserted in an 1873 speech that the Chinese were an inferior race engaged in servile labor, and that they drained the country's treasury by sending their remittances back to their families in China, Gibson responded that it was in the interest of the Catholic Church to oppose Chinese immigration since the Church's own coffers depended upon the contributions of Irish Catholic workers. In response to Bouchard's claim that Chinese servants were driving White women to prostitution, Gibson stated that "Irish Catholic servants were perfectly capable of descending into prostitution

---

[53] Paddison, *American Heathens*, 125.

[54] Many Protestants in the United States saw the *Syllabus of Errors* as presenting an antagonistic relationship between the Catholic Church and the modern world because it "condemned the notion that the Pope should reconcile himself with progress, liberalism, and modern civilization." See Lefebure, *Transforming Interreligious Relations*, 9.

on their own volition and did not require the competition of the Chinese to assist them."[55]

Henceforth, Gibson took a controversial approach in arguing for Chinese immigration by attacking Roman Catholicism, Irish workers, and labor unions. Other pro-Chinese Protestants expanded on this approach by adding alleged Catholic conspiracy theses about the subversion of free American institutions by the Vatican and organized labor.

By 1879, it became clear that the pro-Chinese clergy were having little influence in the Chinese labor and immigration debate as Southern Democrats and Republicans in western states united in support for the restriction of Chinese immigration. The same year, Kearney and his WPC managed to include the discriminatory anti-Chinese labor provisions into the second California state constitution, as noted above. In the end, anti-Chinese factions got the bill passed through Congress, and the stage was set for President Chester Arthur to sign the Chinese Exclusion Act into law on May 6, 1882.

The act also denied citizenship to those who were already in the states, and their wives were made ineligible for entry. To Protestant clergy opposing the Exclusion Act, it became painfully clear that the actual number of Chinese converts to Christianity was pitifully small, and that most Chinese continued to maintain their temples and shrines.[56] Even Gibson, the state's most outspoken champion of the Chinese, by 1881 had embraced Chinese immigration restriction without "abandoning hopes for evangelizing the Chinese or protecting their basic human rights."[57]

---

[55] Andrew Theodore Urban, "An Intimate World: Race, Migration, and Chinese and Irish Domestic Servants in the United States, 1850–1920" (PhD dissertation: University of Minnesota, 2009), 170.

[56] Seager, "Some Denominational Reactions," 59–60.

[57] Paddison, *American Heathens*, 147.

Early Chinese American Civil Rights Activists

While most Chinese were manual laborers with little or no education, there were a few exceptions. Ng Poon Chew, a Chinese convert who became an ordained Protestant minister, used his position to argue against restricting Chinese from entering the United States.[58] As racial resentment intensified in the late 1870s and Chinese in San Francisco found themselves losing their White allies, Chan Pak Kwai, a licensed Methodist preacher sought suffrage for the Chinese to counter the menace of the Irish Catholic votes. At the time when the anti-Chinese movement had overshadowed tensions between Catholics and Protestants, Chan tried to revive the Catholic–Protestant rivalry to support Chinese immigration. Congregationalist lay preachers, Jee Gam and Lem Chung were farsighted in their calls to build bridges between Asian and Black Protestants to counter White Christian nationalism of the time.[59]

One of America's most famous civil rights activists, yet hardly a household name, was Wong Chin Foo. He dedicated his life to advocate for the equal rights of the Chinese. The first to use the label "Chinese American," Wong urged Chinese immigrants to become Americanized and fight for their rights as citizens. He testified before a congressional committee to repeal citizenship denied to the Chinese and to oppose the renewal of the Chinese Exclusion Act.[60] When the Chinese Exclusion Act was about to pass for the second time in 1892 and Congressman Thomas Geary argued for renewing it by imposing new restrictions, Wong established the Chinese Equal Rights League, an

---

[58] Lum, "Religion on the Road," 166.

[59] Paddison, "Anti-Catholicism and Race in Post-Civil War San Francisco," 539–40.

[60] Scott D. Seligman, *The First Chinese American: The Remarkable Life of Wong Chin Foo* (Hong Kong: Hong Kong University Press, 2013).

organization whose purpose was to fight for the civil rights of Chinese immigrants and Chinese Americans. When the Geary Act was passed to extend the exclusion of the Chinese for another ten years, Wong mobilized tens of thousands to protest against the discriminatory legislation. It was "one of the first massive civil disobedience cases in U.S. history."[61] As Scott Seligman writes in *The First Chinese American: The Remarkable Life of Wong Chin Foo*, "He believed deeply in justice, equality, and enfranchisement, and repeatedly challenged Americans to live up to these values that they so freely espoused on the one hand, and so utterly failed to apply to the Chinese on the other."[62]

Another Chinese American who resisted the legislation of an exclusionary law against the Chinese was Yan Phou Lee, a convert to Christianity, graduate of Yale University, and the first native of China to marry an American woman. He was an assimilationist who argued that Chinese are just as capable of becoming good American citizens as are European immigrants. In addition to his autobiography, Yan wrote many essays raising consciousness about the ways in which Chinese immigrants were mistreated in the United States. In the "Other Side of the Chinese Question," he resolutely condemned the hypocrisy that "Californians prohibited the Chinese from becoming citizens and then accused them of failure to become naturalized."[63] In his response to the anti-immigration slogan, "Chinese Must Go!" of Denis Kearney, Yan wrote "The Chinese Must Stay," in which he praised the preamble of the Declaration of Independence explaining that Thomas Jefferson asserted that "all are created equal and made this fair land a refuge

---

[61] Wenxian Zhang, "Standing Up against Racial Discrimination: Progressive Americans and the Chinese Exclusion Act in the Late Nineteenth Century," *Phylon* 56, no. 1 (1960): 9–10.

[62] Seligman, *The First Chinese American*, xi.

[63] Cited in Zhang, "Standing Up against Racial Discrimination," 11.

for the whole world," and then he powerfully denounced "how far this Republic has departed from its high ideal and reversed its traditionary policy [as] may be seen in the laws passed against the Chinese."[64]

In summary, the underlying objective of Kearney's WPC was not simply to advocate for fair wages for White workers but for the Irish to become part of the dominant White ethnic group. To do this, they had to adopt a White supremacist ideology by displaying nativist racism toward the Chinese. In California, Bouchard, Kearney, and members of the WPC identified themselves as patriotic White Christians and sought to keep the state White by persecuting Chinese workers for their race, religion, culture, and personal hygiene. Kearney's sinophobic declaration in the heyday of "sandlot," a vacant field across from the San Francisco City Hall where he gave his racist speeches against the unsuitability of the Chinese to be a part of American society, echoed what Horace Greeley, the founder and editor of the *New York Tribune* had written decades earlier: "The Chinese are uncivilized, unclean, and filthy beyond all conception without any of the higher domestic or social relations; lustful and sensual in their dispositions; every female is a prostitute of the barest order."[65]

Given the opportunity to start a new beginning in western states by joining the elite White racial group, which had excluded them in the East, it is not surprising that among the strongest supporters of the Chinese Exclusion Act were the Irish, as well as the Knights of Labor, an organization with an overwhelming Catholic membership. They did everything in their power to ensure that the Chinese were barred from entering the United States because,

---

[64] Ibid.

[65] In 1854. Stuart Creighton Miller, *The Unwelcome Immigrant: The American Image of the Chinese, 1785–1882* (Berkeley: University of California Press, 1969), 169.

for the Irish Catholics, "America is for Americans"[66]—in other words, America is a White person's country.

Irish immigrants, persecuted for their Catholic faith and racialized as biologically inferior to White Protestants on the East Coast, recognized in California that their physical Whiteness was more salient when juxtaposed to the Chinese. Instead of living out their Catholic faith, they took on the mantle of Whiteness and treated the Chinese as badly as they themselves were treated by the nativist Know-Nothing Party and Anglo-Saxon Whites. The Irish became White by being racist toward the Chinese whom they saw as economic competitors and a threat to their livelihood.

Similarly, they were often actively discriminating against African Americans on the East Coast, as well, separating themselves from their Black counterparts in the adoption of racist views and by opposing the abolitionist movement.[67] Frederick Douglass, an abolitionist and social reformer, noted that the Irish had been taught "to hate and despise the colored people" and adopting racist views toward African Americans was "essential to their own prosperity."[68] Too many Irish, unfortunately, acted as if their American identity was formed by embracing Whiteness, requiring

---

[66] Mary Robert Coolidge, an American sociologist and author, noted an irony in the fissure created between New England reformers and imported Chinese laborers, on the one hand, and Irish and Continental immigrants, on the other: the Yankees, including former Know-Nothings, an anti-Catholic and anti-foreigner political party, defended the Chinese while the Irish demanded "America for the Americans." Kevin Jenks, "Denis Kearney and the Chinese Exclusion Acts," *Straight Thinking on Immigration* 6, no. 3 (Spring 1996): 7.

[67] It is beyond the scope of this volume to discuss anti-Black racism of the Irish. For more information, see Noel Ignatiev, *How the Irish Became White* (New York: Routledge, 2009).

[68] Frederick Douglass, *My Bondage and My Freedom* (New York: Miller, Orton, 1857), 454.

them to treat Chinese and African Americans as the Other. This is a sad narrative often repeated in American history about how the oppressed became the oppressors.

Yellow Peril Today

While the yellow peril myth is the predominant stereotype that shaped the lives of Asian Americans in the past, it has resurfaced during the recent public health crisis to justify hatred and mistreatment of AAPI in the United States. When COVID-19 was first detected in the United States, an Asian American woman wearing a mask on a New York City subway was attacked by another woman who assumed she had coronavirus. A month later, in March 2020, a twenty-three-year-old student from Korea was entering a building in midtown Manhattan when she was grabbed by the hair and punched to the left side of her jaw by another woman for not wearing a mask.[69] It's damned if you do; damned if you don't. In other words, if you look Asian, the assumption is that you must be a carrier of the virus.

On March 23, 2020, Jeff Yang, frequent contributor to CNN Opinion, tweeted his first "breathing while Asian" moment: "Went out for groceries and an older masked White woman passing by the line shouted 'F--K YOU' at me for no apparent reason. As I stared at her, she pulled off her mask, coughed directly at me, turned on her heel and walked off." This woman not only verbally harassed Yang but also committed a hate incident by coughing at him. There have been many such incidents. A viral prejudice that scapegoats any and all Asians as the alleged source of COVID is "a new kind of profiling," says Asian American community activist and author Helen Zia, who dubbed this pattern of hostility "coughing while Asian"; these incidents have become frequent enough to trigger a social media hashtag, #coughingwhileasian.

---

[69] "'Where's Your (Expletive) Mask?': Asian Woman Attacked in Manhattan Hate Crime," *ABC7NY Eyewitness News*, March 11, 2020.

In San Fernando Valley, California, an Asian American teen ended up in the emergency room after being assaulted by bullies in his high school who accused him of having coronavirus. On March 14, 2020, at a Sam's Club in Midland, Texas, a nineteen-year-old Latino suspect stabbed three Burmese American family members, including a two-year-old and a six-year-old, with the assumption that they were infecting people with the virus. This hate crime was also a case of racial profiling; the victims were not Chinese. Although the father and children who were attacked are Chin, an ethnic minority group from Burma, various English-language reports and news sharing on social media conflated Chin with Chinese.

This blurring between nations and ethnicities shows how Asians become a singular race in the United States, targeted and lumped together as scapegoats—a good example of what Robert Chang and Keith Aoki called "xenophobic racism" or "nativistic racism." It is a way to signify how xenophobia or nativism operates in tandem with racism to preserve a conception of the nation in which there is a hegemonic association between Whiteness and Americanness.[70] The reactions of strangers, an older woman, high school bullies, and a young Latino assume Asian Americans are foreign outsiders, which made it easier to cast aspersion and to inflict injury on those they considered as carriers of the COVID-19 virus.

The hate crime committed in Midland, Texas, occurred before former President Trump first tweeted his inflammatory rhetoric, "Chinese Virus," on March 16, 2020, but he had already referred to the new virus as a "China plague" during his first presidential debate on September 29, 2019.[71] From the onset of the pandemic,

---

[70] Robert S. Chang and Keith Aoki, "Centering the Immigrant in the Inter/National Imagination," *California Law Review* 85, no. 5 (1998): 315.

[71] Mishal Reja, "Trump's 'Chinese Virus' Tweet Helped Lead to Rise in Racist and Anti-Asian Twitter Content: Study," *ABC News*, March 18, 2021.

Trump consistently blamed China for its failure to control the pandemic, for the lack of transparency in communicating the origins of COVID-19, and for global recessions while denying his own mishandling in playing down the threat of COVID-19, delays in testing, giving misleading public statements, and carrying out other acts of mismanagement that put thousands of lives at risk. The escalation of blame against China, amplified by political propaganda characterizing COVID-19 as a "Chinese virus" and hashtags such as "Kung-flu" put Asian Americans at risk for hate incidents, including violent assaults.

Researchers found that there was a rise in anti-Asian hashtags and an increase in hate crimes the week after Trump first tweeted the incendiary rhetoric "Chinese Virus" on March 16, 2020. The study further found that anti-Asian hate sentiments increased to 50.4 percent out of 777,852 for those who used hashtags with #Chinesevirus, compared to a 19.7 percent increase out of 495,289 for those who used the #COVID-19 hashtag.[72] Furthermore, the Anti-Defamation League, the world's leading antihate organization, through its Center of Technology and Society showed that twelve hours following Trump's tweet about his and Mrs. Trump's COVID-19 diagnoses, there was an 85 percent increase in anti-Asian language and conspiracy theories tracked on Twitter conversations and activity.[73]

In their insightful article, "Yellow Peril and Techno-Orientalism in the Time of COVID-19," Lok Siu and Claire Chun discuss the ideology of yellow peril articulated through the terrain

---

[72] Yulin Hswen, Xiang Xu, Anna Hing et al., "Association of '#covid19' versus '#chinesevirus' with Anti-Asian Sentiments on Twitter: March 9–23, 2020," *American Public Health Association,* AJPH.Alphapublications.org, January 3, 2021.

[73] "ADL Report: Anti-Asian Hostility Spikes on Twitter after President Trump's COVID Diagnosis," *Anti-Defamation League*, ADL.org, October 9, 2020.

of "techno-Orientalism," the racialized fear of Chinese techno-logical domination, demonstrated by companies like Huawei and TikTok, and how these corporations illustrate "the extension of the 'Chinese virus' trope that already exists in the domains of public health (as biological pathogen) and research institutions (scientist-spy) into the realm of everyday consumer technologies."[74] In short, Trump tapped into the hate sentiment in our society and normalized it by routinely scapegoating China and Chinese people. His repetitive use of ethnic slurs to refer to a new type of coronavirus has given the green light for racists and extremists of all shades to incite hate violence against Asian Americans. Words matter, especially when uttered by the president.

AAPI Health Care Workers

While the devastating stereotype of equating Asian bodies with COVID-19 has been present in nearly every hate incident committed against AAPI, it is painfully experienced by AAPI health care workers who have been targets of anti-Asian bigotry. According to a 2018 report by the Migration Policy Institute, 40 percent of all immigrant health care workers in the United States were from Asia. Of this percentage, 15 percent were physicians and surgeons; 24 percent were registered nurses; and 30 percent consists of all health care support workers. During this pandemic, some of these health care workers experienced rejections from their patients who requested to be treated by non-Asian physicians or nurses. Some have encountered verbal and physical harassment while taking the subway to and from work.

---

[74] Lok Siu and Claire Chun, "Yellow Peril and Techno-orientalism in the Time of COVID-19: Racialized Contagion, Scientific Espionage, and Techno-Economic Warfare," in *Journal of Asian American Studies* 23, no. 3 (October 2020): 434.

Natty Jumreornvong, a medical student of Thai descent, recalled her encounters with racial taunts from psychiatry patients at a New York hospital where she was training. On her way to work, she was spat upon by a bystander who told her to "go back to China" and on another occasion a stranger pulled her hair and physically assaulted her. She reported her story to a local newspaper, which declined to cover it.[75] Dr. Amy Zhang, an anesthesiology resident at the University of Washington, told the *Los Angeles Times* that the escalation of anti-Asian bigotry "makes racism seem a lot scarier than the virus."

The *Washington Post* ran a story about Lucy Li, a twenty-eight-year-old anesthesiology resident at Massachusetts General Hospital who experienced verbal harassment from a stranger who followed her to the subway and discharged a profanity-laced racist outburst at her. Initially, she was stunned and, later, was saddened and angered by the irony, saying, "I'm risking my own personal health, and then to be vilified just because of what I look like."[76] In *Crosscut*, a Pacific Northwest news site, Li wrote, "Despite the fact that I clawed myself out of poverty to chase the American dream, despite the fact that I can and have saved lives under stressful conditions, none of this protects me from racist vitriol."[77] Similar sentiments have been expressed by many other Asian health care workers around the country during the pandemic.

Also, among ethnic groups of health care workers, Filipino nurses working in hospitals and nursing homes are disproportionately impacted by COVID-19. According to the April 2021 survey by National Nurses United, Filipino nurses, while making up only

[75] Michelle Lee, "How a Rally after the Atlanta Shootings Helped Heal Asian American Health Care Workers," *Stat News*, April 3, 2021.
[76] Tracy Jan, "Asian American Doctors and Nurses are Fighting Racism and Coronavirus," *Washington Post,* May 19, 2020.
[77] Quoted in Jennifer Peltz, Asian American Healthcare workers Fight the Coronavirus—And Racist Attacks," *Los Angeles Times*, May 7, 2021.

4 percent of the total registered nurses in the country, represent 30.1 percent of the nurses who died from COVID-19 complications. This represents 48.8 percent of registered nurses of color who have died of COVID-19 and related complications.[78]

Filipino health care workers have played a central role in the US medical system, and they are tied to the complicated history of a colonial relationship between the United States and the Philippines. At the end of the Spanish–American War in 1898, the Philippines became a colony of the United States. The interrelated myths of US exceptionalism and benevolence followed as President William McKinley claimed that "the colonization of the Philippines was a 'benevolent assimilation,' assuring a full measure of individual rights and liberties."[79] Part of a policy of "benevolence" was the creation of American hospitals and nursing schools in the Philippines that produced Filipino nurses to work in the United States rather than in their native country. Concomitant with the creation of an Americanized training hospital system was the establishment of an Americanized education system that further predisposed Filipinos to American cultures and customs.[80]

For a variety of reasons, including a path to a better life and earning enough to send remittances back home, Filipino nurses have been channeled to the United States. Having been trained in an Americanized nursing curriculum, and brought up in an Americanized education system in the Philippines, hospitals in the United States specifically looked for Filipino nurses when there

[78] National Nurses United, "Sins of Omission: How Government Failures to Track Covid-19 Data Have Led to More than 3,200 Health Care Worker Deaths and Jeopardize Public Health," NationalNursesUnited.org, March 2021.

[79] Paulina Cachero, "From AIDS to COVID-19, America's Medical System Has a Long History of Relying on Filipino Nurses to Fight on the Frontlines," *TIME*, May 30, 2021.

[80] Catherine Ceniza Choy, *Empire of Care: Nursing and Migration in Filipino American History* (Durham, NC: Duke University Press, 2003), 4–5.

were nursing shortages, especially during times of health crises. For example, during the HIV/AIDS epidemic in the 1980s, when some US-born health care workers refused to work with AIDS patients, American hospitals turned to Filipino nurses, who migrated to the United States to fill the gaps. The same can be said about the COVID-19 pandemic. Filipino nurses, on the whole, face wage discrimination, and those without permanent residency or US citizenship have been exploited by those with power in health care facilities who force them to work long hours in understaffed hospitals and, sometimes, in unsafe conditions. Because Filipino nurses tend to work in medical/surgical and critical care units, they are at greater risk of falling victim to COVID.[81] Filipino nurses are necessary to keep the American health care system functioning, yet they are often seen as expendable and exploited in the process—subject to the same fate as their Chinese American colleagues, due to racial assumptions and stigmatization.

Stigmatized by the Actions of a Few

The United States has a long history of naturalizing viruses and contagions as being endemic to the bodies of Chinese and other Asians and Pacific Islanders to justify xenophobia and mistreatment. During COVID, they were continually represented in an "Orientalist and racist depiction," exemplified by racist jokes and stereotypes surrounding their "strange and unwholesome eating habits" and consumption of "weird" or "exotic" foods.

I was reminded of this at a dinner in a religious community when a well-respected friar, someone who is sensitive to the struggles of people of color and an ally of their causes, curiously asked me whether anyone in my family ate bat soup. He was neither making a racist joke nor stereotyping what Chinese supposedly

---

[81] Cachero, "From AIDS to COVID-19."

eat, but by personalizing this culinary myth to my family, perhaps the assumption is that consuming bats must be a widespread practice among Chinese and Chinese Americans. This took me back to a memory from many years earlier when a friar in my community, tongue in cheek, told another friar who had a dog that I was thinking of having dog for supper. While these are compassionate people who meant no harm or malice and who had neither nativist nor xenophobic intentions, their unsuspecting characterization of the Chinese as dog eaters and consumers of bat soup resurfaces an enduring trope that unconsciously reinforces the Othering of Asian Americans. Their inquiries also constitute a dissemination of microaggressive stereotypes into public speech and a perpetuation of a worldview that Chinese and Asian Americans are outside of American norms of morality and culture.

Although the practice of eating dog meat is not common in China, there are some Chinese in mainland China who eat dogs and still a few who eat bats. Perhaps, they picked up this perceived "uncivilized" habit during the many famines in mainland China throughout its history. In 2020, the Agriculture Ministry of China reclassified dogs as companion animals but did not outright prohibit the consumption of dog meat. The cities Shenzhen and Zhuhai in the southern province of Guangdong went a step further by becoming the first Chinese cities to outlaw dog meat sales and consumption.[82] This is a small victory for animal activists, celebrities, and young Chinese citizens who, for years, have sought to terminate the practice of dog eating and to end the annual Yulin summer solstice event called the "Lychee and Dog Meat Festival."

So, when memes and images of Chinese people eating bats went viral on social media in the United States, many Asian Americans knew that they would be viewed as consumers of bats

---

[82] Grace Qi, "China's Annual Dog Meat Festival Is Underway, but Activists Hope It Will Be the Last," *CBS News*, June 24, 2020.

and rodents. The mainstream media often covers these atypical eating habits as a characteristic of all Chinese. In contrast, when poor Whites in the rural South are looked down upon by the general population for consuming squirrel, raccoon, and possum, White Americans across the country would not be stigmatized for the food habits of the rural South subculture. As long as White privilege exists, it is difficult for Asian Americans or other people of color to access the privileges of "individualism" that the culture promotes and cherishes.

Conclusion and Theological Reflection

We have looked at some of the ways in which the ideology of White supremacy has operated through the yellow peril stereotype. Chinese laborers were seen as carriers of contagion and unfair competitors to White workers in the labor market, but nowhere is the operation of White supremacy more evident than the depiction of Chinese laborers as "heathen." Their heathenism, associated with their "pagan customs" and "superstitious religion," was often cited for their inability to assimilate into a White Christian nation.

This shows up most prominently in the practice of "secondary burial." In Guangdong, China, where most of the Chinese laborers came from, some villagers "practiced 'secondary burial,' in which the dead were first buried in a shallow grave, exhumed after a few years so that the decomposing flesh could be removed, and then the bones reburied in an auspicious location."[83] It does not require much imagination to see how ghastly and repulsive this practice must have been to Westerners. In addition, the secondary burial was very difficult to perform by the Chinese laborers on the West Coast when their jobs required them to be on the move in a landscape unfamiliar to them and "under the control of often hostile European

---

[83] Lum, "Religion on the Road," 161.

Americans who dictated where the railroad would go and where the Chinese could be buried, often outside 'white cemeteries.'"[84] Moreover, it is in the practice of secondary burials that the intimate connection between land and kinship shows up most prominently. Chinese migrants were willing to spend their hard-earned money to ship back the bones of the deceased to China, where they could be buried in a favorable location and where the soul of the deceased could be venerated by family members.

These sorts of "intractable" religious and cultural differences led to blatant White supremacist sermons and speeches delivered by Bouchard, Kalloch, Kearney, Sargent, and others about the impossibility for the pagan Chinese to become Christian. The underlying assumption was that one had to become more White in order to become a Christian. They could not see the Chinese as fully human much less the presence of Christ in them.

In contrast, Reverends William Speer and Otis Gibson and other pro-Chinese Protestant clergy sought to assimilate the Chinese into American society through conversion to Christianity. As Timothy Tseng argues in his chapter, "Beyond Orientalism," that "mission and evangelism were promoted as the primary vehicles of incorporation of Asians into American society" from the earliest Protestant encounters with the Chinese in the 1850s. By the late nineteenth century, Protestant faith in Asian assimilation "was both a humanitarian response to the victims of American racism and a hope that the failure to fully 'Christianize' the 'Oriental in America' would find eventual success in their gradual and natural assimilation into American society."[85]

---

[84] Ibid.

[85] Timothy Tseng, "Beyond Orientalism and Assimilation: The Asian American as Historical Subject," in *Realizing the America of Our Hearts: Theological Voices of Asian Americans*, ed. Fumitaka Matsuoka and Eleazar S. Fernandez (Nashville, TN: Chalice Press, 2003), 66.

The evangelism and activism of pro-Chinese Protestant clergy reflected the Catholic Social Teaching (CST) principles of common good and respect for human dignity as they sought to protect the Chinese migrants' basic human rights, doing everything they possibly could to resist the legislation that would bar the Chinese from entering the United States. Meanwhile, Irish immigrants, who also faced racial and religious bigotry, however qualitatively different from that encountered by the Chinese, took advantage of these yellow peril depictions of the Chinese by casting themselves as defenders of White Christian America. Thus, they exhibited nativist racism toward the Chinese in order to improve their position in the racial hierarchy. And sadly, the yellow peril stereotype that shaped the lives of Chinese workers in the past has resurfaced in its contemporary form during the present novel coronavirus pandemic.

In a civilized society, all members, especially those from vulnerable populations, should not be fearful about doing the things they need to do for survival and to live a full and healthy life. They should not be afraid to go to the grocery store, to keep their doctor appointments, to take public transportation, or go for a leisurely walk around their neighborhood for fear of being verbally harassed or physically assaulted because of their ancestry or the way God has created them. This is what makes the virus of hate and racism accompanying COVID-19 so despicable and dangerous. The moral virus of hate and racism has been a part of the United States since its foundation, and anti-Asian racism has existed even before the Chinese arrived in significant numbers in the mid-nineteenth century. What COVID-19 has done is brought to the surface the sins of our past that we have not adequately dealt with: the continued portrayals of Chinese and other Asians as perpetual foreign Others whose religions, cultures, and ways of life have been considered so different from those of the dominant group that they are seen as unassimilable and a yellow peril threat to the American way of life. These historical forms of racism and xenophobia continue to persist to this day as COVID-19 is associated with anyone who is perceived as Chinese.

During this pandemic, the moral virus of hate and racism is spreading faster than the public health crisis caused by a biological pathogen. These hate incidents, many of which are tracked and collected by Stop AAPI Hate include verbal harassment, shunning, physical assault, coughing at or spitting upon, and barring from an establishment and transportation. These incident reports reflect the visceral reaction of many Americans when faced with the fear of contracting a virus over which they have little control. Instead of educating themselves on the situation, they allow their personal prejudice, xenophobic hysteria, and anxiety about the unknown to dictate their behavior. In so doing, they reveal the cruel forces of racism and intolerance that pervade our society, adding to AAPI's agony and suffering.

To give a snapshot of how incidents of racism directed at Asian Americans during COVID-19 correlate with xenophobic statements about China and Chinese people, Russell Jeung, Melissa Borja, and other researchers at Stop AAPI Hate analyzed 1,843 incidents of racism reported from March 19 to May 13, 2020, of which 502 or 27.2 percent of respondents shared that "China" or "Chinese" were said as part of the attack. Xenophobic comments regarding China are further broken down into content categories. Examples from an incident report reflect each of these six content categories:

1. Virulent animosity: "Person called me a 'yellow n----r' and yelled 'go back to China, bitch!'"
2. Scapegoating of China: "As I was taking a brief walk for fresh air and exercise, a random person on the opposite side of the street screamed at me "Go f—king die, you chink! All you chinks brought us the Chinese virus!"

3. Anti-immigrant nationalism: "A White male walked by me and said, 'you f—king Chinese spread the coronavirus to this country, you should all leave this country!' I was alone when this happened."

4. China as the enemy: "While I was at the grocery store, another patron referred to me as 'another one of those damn Chinese trying to infect everyone in the community.'"

5. Parroting of "Chinese Virus" term: "A car of men was driving around Chicago targeting Asians, yelling racial slurs, shouting 'Chinese Virus,' 'get out of America' and fake sneezing. They even blasted a rap song about the virus that blames the Chinese and 'how dirty they are.'"

6. Orientalist and racist depictions: "This particular incident involved two of my students. One of them is Chinese and the other student was teasing him, saying that he had Coronavirus and telling the other students to not go near him. Another student claimed that Chinese people eat baby dogs and bats and that's how the virus spread."[86]

Two common themes thread through all the above incidents: (1) a foreign outsider and then a more devastating stereotype (2) equating Chinese, or those who are perceived to be Chinese, with the novel coronavirus.

For "virulent animosity" and "anti-immigrant nationalism," almost every Asian or Asian American is familiar with statements like "Go back to China!" or "You should leave the country!" as painful examples of racist attacks that express a range of hostility that spans from spiteful animosity to anti-immigrant racism. "Scapegoating of China," "China as enemy," "parroting of 'Chinese Virus'," and "Orientalist and racial depictions" are in one way or another equating Chinese or Asian Americans with COVID-

---

[86] Melissa Borja, Russell Jeung, Aggie Yellow Horse, et al., "Anti-Chinese Rhetoric Tied to Racism against Asian Americans," *STOP AAPI Hate*, June 17, 2020, https://stopaapihate.org/anti-chinese-rhetoric-tied-to-racism-against-asian-americans/.

19. Indeed, at the heart of the protest against anti-Asian racism in Europe and the United States is a protest against the ignorant assumption that because the novel coronavirus first appeared in Wuhan, China, then all Chinese around the world must be infected with it. This protest is aptly summarized up by the political slogan, "My ethnicity is not a virus." This was inspired by French Asians who initiated a community of resistance to racist incidents on public transportation and elsewhere by sharing the hashtag *#JeNeSuisPasUnVirus*, or "I am not a virus," widely on social media.

The hashtag "I am not a virus" is not simply resisting anti-Asian racism in Europe and the United States but challenges the dehumanization of Asians and Asian Americans that occurs when we are associated with a vector of disease and death. It challenges the idea of equating a human being to a virus, an unconscious thing. The proclamation "I am not a virus" then lends itself to the human conscious, expressing inner feelings, emotions, warmth, and humanity. We declare "I am not a virus" because we have feelings, emotions, warmth, and humanity; we experience love, joy, and ecstasy, as well as alienation, hurt, and suffering.

We also are not a virus because we are created in the image and likeness of God. As Pope John Paul II reminds us in *Redemptor Hominis*, solicitude for human dignity and rights stands at the heart of an authentic understanding of incarnational Christology. We do not have to prove that we are humans. Our worth and dignity as human beings are God-given rights. To resist the dehumanization of being equated with a virus, we need to reclaim our identity as people living in a society in which we are Americans of Asian descent. Unless we reclaim our dignity as human beings and refuse to be reduced to viruses and perpetual foreign Others, we will be forever aliens in our own country.[87] This cannot be done solely by

---

[87] Joseph Cheah, "Life in the Fishbowl: An Asian American Autobiographical Theological Reflection," in *Envisioning Religion, Race, and Asian*

our own efforts. We need to work in solidarity with other people of color and White allies to confront and overcome, once and for all, the source, depth, and pervasiveness of the virus of hate and racism in our society. The principle of solidarity of CST is exercised when all of us recognize the essential bond that exists between all persons who are created in the image and likeness of God.

In their statement against harassment and racial discrimination suffered by AAPI during COVID-19, the bishops of the US Conference of Catholic Bishops have publicly condemned any attitude or behavior that does not respect the dignity of another human being. They called on "Catholics, fellow Christians and all people of good will to help stop all racially motivated discriminatory actions and attitudes, for they are attacks against human life and dignity and are contrary to Gospel values."[88] The notion that human dignity as the grounding for human rights is a birthright for all people is stressed in the Vatican document, *Dignitatis Humanae* (Declaration of Religious Freedom). Indeed, the desire to be recognized as humans rather than viruses requires no rationale. It is our fundamental God-given right that AAPI be recognized and respected as human beings. To do otherwise is to go against the mystery and sacredness of the human person God has created. Conversely, to disavow the view that AAPI are viruses and less than human is to discover the inherent dignity of AAPI as persons in Christ.

Americans, ed. David K. Yoo and Khyati Y. Joshi (Honolulu: University of Hawaii Press, 2020), 202.

[88] US Conference of Catholic Bishops, "Bishop Chairmen Condemn Racism and Xenophobia in the Context of the Coronavirus Pandemic," USCCB.org, May 5, 2020.

2

Model Minority Myth

After my brief presentation on "Anti-Asian Racism and Xenophobia in the Wake of COVID-19" at the May 4, 2020, meeting of faculty at the University of Saint Joseph, a number of colleagues asked me to do a webinar with a fuller version of my talk. Later that month, however, on May 25, the slow horrific lynching of George Floyd went viral, and the systemic racism experienced by African Americans, previously so coded that many non-Black Americans might not crack the cipher, descended upon all Americans like a bolt from the blue. This awakened the moral consciousness of Americans from all ethnicities and walks of life to do what is right by standing up for the Black Lives Matter Movement and denouncing systemic racism and immoral practices.

As we witness another occurrence of a reckoning on race and a possible transformation in American society, it would be presumptuous of me to give my original talk without connecting to the matter that has been uppermost in the minds and hearts of most Americans since George Floyd's murder. This is why this chapter comes from the talks on anti-Asian racism and violence that I have given since June 1, 2020. It examines the role of the model minority myth in the racial positioning of Asian Americans in the dynamic of the Black/White relationship, and how this myth goes against the original meaning of justice articulated in the pastoral letter against racism.

A Model Based on a Fallacy

The model minority myth relies on division as its guiding principle, and leads those attributed with the myth to a sense of isolation and a precarious power. It is based on a fallacy that the American dream is readily attainable by all—even by those with histories of oppression; if we keep our heads down, work hard, and are self-reliant in our pursuits, then we can achieve anything we desire.

Historically, this view achieved canonical status in the doctrine of Manifest Destiny: the colonial notion that the future of this land is golden because God has blessed its way of life, the noblest in creation, ordaining it to spread the blessing throughout the continent, even by means of conquest and dispossessing the land of the original inhabitants. This presumed mandate can be traced to a series of fifteenth-century papal bulls, which would later be known as the doctrine of discovery or, more accurately, the Doctrine of Christian Discovery, which granted rulers of Christian nations the permission to take possession of territories not already claimed by another Christian country.[1] At its core, it says that the future is golden and that a golden future is readily attainable to all because nothing can frustrate the divine mandate except diffidence in the selection of means for its fulfillment.

By the late 1960s, this aspect of Manifest Destiny found definitive expression in the model minority myth ascribed to Asian Americans as hardworking, law-abiding, and successful. The media proliferated this image of Asian Americans as the model minority beginning in the mid-1960s, and throughout the '70s, and '80s. Painted as Horatio Alger figures by the media, Asian Americans were seen as persistently pursuing the American dream, silently

---

[1] Leo D. Lefebure, *Transforming Interreligious Relations: Catholic Responses to Religious Pluralism in the United States* (Maryknoll, NY: Orbis Books, 2020), 67.

overcoming their minority status, and "fully participating in American society with its attendant economic benefits."[2]

The educational, economic, and professional achievements of Asian Americans were considered proof that independent assimilation of a minority group was possible without special programs (such as affirmative action) and other forms of assistance from the government.[3] While the popularity of the model minority myth originated with the publication of the 1966 *New York Times* article "Success Story, Japanese-American Style" by William Pettersen,[4] historian Ellen Wu, in her book *The Color of Success*, traces the narrative to Chinese and Japanese Americans who sought respectability in the 1940s' racist society by portraying themselves as having the right culture and family values, and by serving their country during the Second World War, to be worthy of respect and dignity in the eyes of all Americans. To win allies in the Cold War, however, the narrative of Asian Americans as a model minority was co-opted by neoconservatives and liberal politicians to present the United States as a racial democracy and rightful leader of the free world. In the 1960s, anxieties about the Civil Rights Movement prompted both neoconservatives and liberal politicians to further portray Asian Americans in a positive light, thereby driving a racial wedge between them and other minoritized groups.[5]

---

[2] Ki-Taek Chun, "The Myth of Asian American Success and Its Educational Ramifications," in *The Asian American Educational Experience: A Source Book for Teachers and Students*, ed. Don T. Nakanishi and Tina Yamano Nishida (New York: Routledge, 1995), 97.

[3] Deborah Woo, *Glass Ceilings and Asian Americans* (Walnut Creek, CA: AltaMira Press, 2000), 25.

[4] William Pettersen, "Success Story, Japanese-American Style," *New York Times Magazine*, January 9, 1966, 20.

[5] Emily Wu, *The Color of Success: Asian Americans and the Origin of the Model Minority* (Princeton, NJ: Princeton University Press, 2015), 165, 171–72.

The model minority myth pits Asian Americans against African Americans in particular because the function of the myth is to show that institutionalized racism is not an insurmountable barrier. Asian Americans are seemingly able to overcome it through hard work, education, and steadfast faith in liberal democracy, as opposed to political protest and self-determination pursued by African Americans. As successive depictions of Asian Americans as nonthreatening and law-abiding citizens took root, they became more acceptable to White Americans. This provided Asian Americans opportunities for social mobility, as they were no longer excluded from access to education and nonmanagerial white-collar jobs, as in the past, and were seen as the "good minority"—educated people with good jobs and strong family bonds.

The popular perception is that education plays a central role in the success of Asian Americans. However, according to Brown University economist Nathaniel Hilger, even before the 1965 Naturalization Act that gave preference to the arrivals of highly educated immigrants to the United States, Asian Americans had already closed the wage gap with Whites. The 1940 census indicated that Asian Americans in California earned less than California-born Black men. But the 1970 census tells us that Asian Americans were, by then, earning about the same as Whites. Hilger's research reveals that there was no significant shift in educational attainments among Asian Americans during this thirty-year period. Rather, the portrayal of Asian Americans as a model minority over the years has removed some structural barriers of discrimination and provided opportunities for White adjacency and social mobility.[6]

Indeed, stories abound about Asian Americans graduating from prestigious universities prior to the Second World War who

---

[6] Jeff Guo, "The Real Secret to Asian American Success Was Not Education," *Washington Post*, November 19, 2016.

nevertheless could not find a professional position in their field of expertise. In his landmark book, *Strangers from a Different Shore*, historian Ronald Takaki recounted a story of a Chinese American graduate from the Massachusetts Institute of Technology who could not secure a job in his field and ended up working as a waiter in a Chinese restaurant. During the Second World War, when the California aircraft industry was desperate for skilled and semiskilled workers, "five thousand young Chinese in San Francisco seemed to have 'no future worthy of their education,' destined instead to 'washing dishes, carrying trays, ironing shirts, cutting meat, drying fish, and selling herbs.'"[7] In other words, Asian Americans were successful not necessarily because we were able to pull ourselves up by our own bootstraps, so to speak, but because we were allowed to succeed for geopolitical reasons during the Cold War.

Since the Civil Rights era, our perceived success has been used as a racial wedge against other people of color, African Americans in particular, to keep White America from having to acknowledge the systemic racism that has prevented the advancement of African Americans. The model minority is based on a fallacy that asserts economic equality can be achieved by recourse to one's own efforts rather than addressing social and racial inequalities for all people of color at structural and systemic levels. Cathy Park Hong did not mince words about the place that Asian Americans occupy when she wrote, "In the popular imagination, Asian Americans inhabit a vague purgatorial status: not white enough nor black enough; distrusted by African Americans, ignored by whites, unless we're being used by whites to keep the black man down."[8]

With division as the guiding principle, the model minority is based on a divide-and-conquer strategy, designed to keep

---

[7] Ronald Takaki, *Strangers from a Different Shore* (New York: Back Bay Books, 1998), 266–67.

[8] Cathy Park Hong, *Minor Feelings: An Asian American Reckoning* (New York: One World, 2020), 9.

the structure of White supremacy intact. As such, it has detrimental effects on the lives of Asian Americans—both in how they perceive themselves and how others perceive them. In terms of the former, it is difficult for some or many to see themselves as the model minority in part because the Asian American community is hardly the monolithic, seamless group that is often portrayed in the American imagination. In reality, the Asian American community is incredibly diverse, representing nearly fifty ethnic groups from over twenty countries in East and Southeast Asia and the Indian subcontinent. It is also a community with the widest income gap of any ethnic group in the United States. In terms of socioeconomic measure, based on 2019 PEW data, two Asian origin groups with the highest household incomes are Indian Americans ($119,000) and Filipino Americans ($90,400), compared with the average income of all US households ($61,800). In contrast, the income of Burmese Americans ($44,400) was less than half that of Filipino Americans. The poverty rates of some Asian origin groups were as high or higher than the US average in 2019. Among Asian groups, Mongolians (25 percent) had the highest poverty rates and Indians (6 percent) the lowest.[9] By lumping the Burmese, Bhutanese, and Hmong as part of the model minority when many, if not all of them came to the United States as refugees (as in the case of Hmong), their economic and educational needs have gone unmet. Besides the economic and educational achievements of selected immigrants and their children, Asian Americans have continued to experience xenophobia, racism, discrimination, hate crimes, verbal harassment, violent physical assaults, and other indicators of a marginalized population rather than one of a model minority.

The myth also says that Asian Americans are a model minority not for majority Whites, but rather for other people of color.

---

[9] Abby Budiman and Neil G. Ruiz, "Key Facts about Asian Americans, a Diverse and Growing Population," *PEW Research Center*, April 29, 2021.

Hence, it is designed for other people of color to perceive Asian Americans as largely politically silent and, therefore, worthy of emulation. It portrays Asian Americans as quiet, hardworking, successful, and assimilating. The implication is that if a minoritized group remains silent and works hard, they will overcome all barriers and achieve upward mobility in American society. This was a way for neoconservatives in the 1960s to redirect the frustration of "failing" minority groups toward Asian Americans while keeping the White establishment from having to acknowledge systemic racism. This resulted in de facto segregation and urban disenfranchisement, preventing also the advancement of Latinx and African Americans.

Because the myth implies that Asian Americans have overcome personal and institutional racism, the assumption is that we must not experience racism and discrimination today. This idea is sometimes expressed disparagingly as *What do they [Asian Americans] have to complain about? They are successful and don't experience racism.*

Connecticut Representative Mike Winkler made this sort of astonishingly ignorant remark in a virtual hearing at the wake of the shooting of three Atlanta massage spas that took the lives of six Asian women when he asserted, "Asians have never been discriminated against."[10] This kind of unacceptable comment is contradicted in the 2019 PEW study, conducted before the COVID-19 pandemic, which showed that 75 percent of Asian Americans indicated that they have experienced discrimination or been treated unfairly because of their race. This compares to 76 percent for Blacks and 58 percent for Hispanics. In contrast, a Hill-HarrisX Poll, released also in 2019, found that most people do not think Asian Americans face a significant amount of discrimination.

---

[10] Mike Pazniokas, "Legislator, Opposing Segregation, Claims Asians 'Have Never Been Discriminated Against'," *Connecticut News Project*, CTMirror.org, March 23, 2021.

Such a marked discrepancy in how Asian Americans perceive themselves and how others in American society perceive them reveals that most Americans hardly know anything about Asian American history and their experience of racism. This makes the model minority a dangerous myth because it denies the existence of present-day racism and discrimination against Asian Americans. This danger is better understood in the context of different subordinations in which Blacks and non-Black minorities are racially positioned in the United States.

Racial Positioning

Two approaches are helpful in understanding the racial positioning of Asian Americans in relation to the ordering of racial groups along the vertical and horizontal axes. The Black/White binary is situated along the vertical axis, whereas the insider/outsider binary is framed along the horizontal axis. The Black/White binary is centered on race in which White people are at the apex of the racial hierarchy, and Black slaves and their descendants are at the bottom. Asians and Latinx are often privileged over Blacks in this racial hierarchy of the Black/White continuum.

For example, even when the Chinese were racialized as "Black" or "non-White" in many legal precedents—for example, the inadmissibility of legal testimony of Chinese against Whites in *People v. Hall* (1854), naturalization requests in *Ah Yup* (1878), school segregation in *Gong Lum v. Rice* (1927), antimiscegenation law between Whites and Asians in Nevada (1861), and fourteen additional states thereafter, just to name a few—they were not seen as property in the same way that Blacks were. With the exception of Chinese women who were brought to the United States as slaves, Chinese and other Asians were considered the alien Other, not fully able to become full legal subjects or citizens (e.g., testifying in court, owning property) or human (e.g., Chinese were considered to be racially and culturally inferior in nineteenth-century America) in the same terms as Whites.

Hence, a better approach in understanding the racial positioning of Asian Americans is not through the racial hierarchy model of the Black/White binary but with an insider/outsider binary, centered on citizenship, where Asian Americans are seen as either perpetual foreigners or a model minority. In other words, although Asian Americans and African Americans shared similar experiences of racial subordination in US history, they were often operating under two different binaries: the Black/White binary in which African Americans were denigrated as property and subhuman, and the insider/outsider binary in which Asian Americans were denigrated as outsiders within the insider/outsider spectrum. Additional examples of the insider/outsider binary include ideas that the Chinese were unassimilable both racially and culturally to the American way of life and that they were unfair competitors who posed a threat to White laborers, combined with the nativist fear that they would outnumber the Whites. This led to the enactment of the Chinese Exclusion Act in 1882, which constructed the Chinese as permanent outsiders who were barred from entering the United States because of their race and nationality.

The fear that the Chinese would outnumber Whites was completely unfounded. To ensure that the Chinese would not populate California, it was very difficult for Chinese women to immigrate in the nineteenth century. In *Strangers from a Different Shore*, Takaki provides us with a lopsided statistic: In 1852, for every Chinese woman in the United States, there were 1,685 Chinese men. By 1870, the ratio of Chinese women to men improved dramatically to fourteen to one.[11] Nonetheless, the gender ratios were skewed enough that many Chinese men who

---

[11] Takaki, *Strangers from a Different Shore*, 121.

wanted to start families had little choice but to return to China to look for a soul mate.

Many Chinese women who came to the United States, however, were victims of sex trafficking. They did not come voluntarily, but were brought to the United States by large syndicates as sex slaves. They had been in bondage since a young age, sometimes even infancy, to be sold as prostitutes. In *Driven Out: The Forgotten War against Chinese Americans*, Jean Pfaelzer details this: "After the Exclusion Act of 1882, a one-year-old girl cost a hundred dollars, a girl of fourteen…cost twelve hundred. . . . During her time as a bond servant, she earned no wages, was not free to leave her 'employer,' was usually overworked, often suffered physical abuse from her mistress, and was sexually available to her master or his son."[12] Because the Thirteenth Amendment banned indentured contracts, buyers circumvented it by paying the purchase money to a Chinese prostitute, who then turned it over to her new owner, as she marked or signed a contract indenturing herself for a predetermined number of years. A typical contract reads:

> If, in that time, I am sick one day, two weeks shall be added to my time; and if more than one day, my term of prostitution shall continue an additional month. But if I run away from the custody of my keeper, then I am to be held as a slave for life.

Since sickness included periods of menstruation, the length of a prostitute's contract was inevitably extended indefinitely. Despite the abolition of slavery, the sale of humans endured in the West.[13] Chinese women who were brought to the United States as prostitutes did not fit neatly within the insider/outsider spectrum that

---

[12] Jean Pfaelzer, *Driven Out: The Forgotten War against Chinese Americans* (New York: Random House, 2007), 94.

[13] Ibid., 95.

Chinese men and other Asians were racially positioned in. These women were certainly outsiders, but they were also treated more like Black slaves, as property and subhuman. Hong puts it graphically in *Minor Feelings*, "I cannot fathom being a fifteen-year-old girl from China abducted and smuggled to this wild barbaric country, locked in a boarding house to be raped ten times a day until her body was hollowed out by syphilis. After that, she was dumped out on the streets to die alone."[14]

From the perspective of Catholic Social Teaching (CST), the sex trafficking of Chinese women is a violation of the dignity of women articulated in Genesis 2, which tells us that women are not possessions to be exploited but are people with equal dignity as men. In the New Testament, Jesus found such dehumanizing treatment of women simply intolerable. He denounced the tradition of treating women as mere possessions (Mk 10:2–12), just as he denounced such treatment of any human being because all human persons, as Genesis 2 reminds us, are from one flesh, created by God to be companions and to be stewards for the created life (Gn 2:15–24).

The Immigration and Nationality Act of 1965, which created immigration preferences based on family reunification and professional skill, has played a significant role in where Asian immigrants lie in the Black/White continuum. The professional skill provision is a "brain drain" policy that attracted the best and the brightest from countries of origin. Many of these selective immigrants have the means and employment to resettle in White suburbs where good schools are located for their children. They are racially positioned above African Americans because they fit into the mold cast by the model minority myth. Unbeknownst to many of them, they are recipients of a divide-and-conquer tactic that was designed to keep Black people at the bottom of the Black/White binary. In contrast, Burmese, Bhutanese, Hmong, and other Asian refugees

---

[14] Hong, *Minor Feelings*, 20.

who resettled in impoverished areas, where poor Black and Brown Americans live, have faced competition over limited resources, police brutality, and more recently, the deportation of Southeast Asian refugees during the Trump administration. They are racially positioned near Blacks since they are treated more like Black citizens than White. Burmese, Vietnamese, and other Southeast Asian Americans do not dominate the popular perceptions of Asian identity in America, yet they constitute more than a quarter of the Asian American population. They, along with Native Americans, are often left out in most discussions of poverty and racism. Thus, depending on whether Asian Americans are wealthy, educated immigrants or poor, uneducated refugees, they may be racially positioned as either close to White or near Black.

The insider/outsider binary tells us that Asian Americans can gain an insider status by becoming "honorary Whites," or they can be grouped together with Latinx as perpetual foreigners. But the Asian American status as either model minority or honorary White is conditional. It can be taken away any time because Asian Americans were historically racialized as "Black" and, today, they are still considered as outsiders. Anti-Asian racism that has surfaced with COVID-19 only serves to remind us that Asian Americans are still seen as forever foreigners.

Case Study:
Racial Positionings of Black and Asian Americans

Two incidents that went viral on social media in 2020 provide good examples of how race/racism is experienced differently by members in Black and Asian American communities and how they are racially positioned in American society. In the first incident, which took place on May 25, 2020, the same day when the murder of George Floyd went viral, Amy Cooper, a young White woman, was walking her dog without a leash in New York's Central Park where leashes are required. An African American man, Christian Cooper, a bird watcher, no relation to Amy Cooper, asked her to put a leash on her dog in accordance with park regulations. In response, she called the police, stating multiple times that a Black man was threatening her and her dog. By focusing on the race of Christian Cooper in her reporting to the police, Amy Cooper demonstrated her White privilege by assuming police would back her up, even though she was clearly the one in the wrong. She exploited a system of White supremacy that could have placed Christian Cooper's life in danger because Black men are often perceived as dangerous in American society, and there are possible dire consequences associated with police contact with Black men in this country. Bryan Massingale, theologian at Fordham University, states, "She assumed that she could exploit deeply ingrained white fears of black men, and she assumed that she could use these deeply ingrained white fears to keep a black man in his place."[15] In a sense, she was weaponizing White fragility[16] to bring about state or communal violence against Black bodies—the sort of racial violence that occurred many times in African American history, including the brutal murder of four-teen-year-old Emmett Till in Mississippi in 1955.

The second incident took place on October 30, 2020, when Amara Walker, CNN correspondent and fill-in anchor, experienced within the span of forty-five minutes to an hour three successive

---

[15] Regina Munch, "Interview with Bryan Massingale: Worship of a False God," *Commonweal*, December 27, 2020.

[16] White fragility is a term coined by Robin DiAngelo. She defines it as "a state in which even a minimum amount of racial stress becomes intolerable, triggering a range of defensive moves. These moves include the outward display of emotions such as anger, fear, and guilt, and behavior such as argumentation, silence, and leaving the stress-inducing situation." See Robin DiAngelo, *White Fragility: Why It's So Hard for White People to Talk about Racism* (Boston: Beacon Press, 2018).

racist encounters at the New Orleans International Airport. In the first encounter, an older man went out of his way, lowered his mask, and uttered, "Ni Hao. ching chong" to Walker who is a Korean American. The phrase "ching chong" is a racial slur considered derogatory due to its historical usage in negatively depicting Chinese speech patterns. Walker was offended by the encounter but kept on walking. Later, at a store, she saw him standing in line right behind her. When she questioned him on whether he knew if what he did was wrong, he gave her a smug look and denied the whole encounter and walked away. In the next encounter, occurring about thirty minutes later, a young man came up to Walker questioning her ability to speak English while she was sitting at a terminal. Her immediate response was to question him on why he would assume she does not speak English. Instead of responding to her question, the young man ridiculed her by uttering gibberish that sounded like "fabricated Asian language" to Walker. When asked to leave, the man started to get disruptive, which is when her producer called security to report the harassment that Walker was facing. The third encounter began with the arrival of the security officer at the scene. Instead of defusing the situation, the officer questioned whether the young man had harassed Walker and started to yell at her and her producer by stating emphatically, "That was not racist! OK? Asking if she speaks English is not racist, OK? Do you understand me?" The security officer gave the impression that Walker's safety was deemed less important than for the young man to approach and harass her. The use of a blatantly ethnic slur portrays, in the first instance, the assumption that a person with an Asian face does not speak English; and, second, the ignorance of the security officer reflects how Asian Americans are seen as perpetual foreigners.

Both the incident in Central Park and the series of incidents that took place at New Orleans International Airport demonstrate the operation of White privilege against minoritized groups. They are similar in that both Asian and African Americans are treated as *Other* in our society. When Amy Cooper called the police and complained that a Black man was threatening her, she exploited a racial stereotype that Black men are dangerous. When Amara Walker encountered men at the airport who mocked her and asked whether she spoke English, they did so out of a racist assumption that people with Asian features cannot be American or native English speakers. As a Black man, Christian Cooper was perceived as a threat, whereas an Asian American woman, Amara Walker, was seen as a foreigner. Neither position is acceptable, but it is important to point out that Black and Asian people are racialized differently in the United States.

The difference stems from the positions African and Asian Americans are placed at in comparison to Whites. African Americans are placed in the bottom of the Black/White binary, where they are seen as inferior to Whites, whereas Asian Americans are placed on an insider/outsider spectrum, where they are perceived as either perpetual foreigners or a model minority or both at the same time—as in the case of Amara Walker. As a journalist and a fill-in anchor for CNN, Walker fits the image of the model minority in the American imagination, yet she is still seen by the first two men as a foreign-born outsider, even though she was born in the United States with English as her native language. In other words, regardless of our actual citizenship status, Asian Americans can slip into a foreign-born outsider status simply by the way we look. The construction of Asian Americans as foreign-born outsiders is what Angelo Ancheta calls "foreigner racialization."[17] We see this racialization in the chart below, where the vertical "color axis" operates to position Blacks as inferior to Whites, whereas the horizontal

---

[17] Angelo N. Ancheta, *Race, Rights, and the Asian American Experience* (New Brunswick, NJ: Rutgers University Press, 2006), 63.

"citizenship axis" operates to cast Asian Americans as foreign-born outsiders, which includes Latinx and Arab Americans or what Neil Gotanda calls "Other non-Whites."[18]

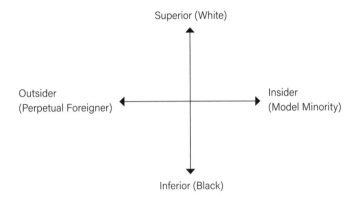

Although these two incidents have differences, with a closer, look one can see that they are similar as well. Whether it is a Black or an Asian person, White society often perceives them as second-class citizens. When Amy Cooper called the police, she knew that in a society that reinforces White privilege and systemic racism, she would have the upper hand in the eyes of the authorities. In the case of Walker, systemic racism among those serving in law enforcement was confirmed when a security officer who was supposed to defuse the situation instead was dismissive of their grievance and verbally censured Walker and her producer. The officer used his power to intimidate them and "re-educate" them on what is and is not racist. In both episodes, the perpetrators exhibited racist behaviors without being afraid of the consequences of their actions. They were emboldened to act in calculated manners because they felt they could get away with their actions. And because racism has a systemic nature, racist individuals often are protected by the system

---

[18] Neil Gotanda, "'Other Non-Whites' in American Legal History: A Review of Justice at War," *Columbia Law Review* 85, no. 5 (1985): 1186.

and, therefore, rarely face proper consequences. This further illustrates that racist behavior is not just considered normal but is often
justified. A misdemeanor charge faced by Amy Cooper for falsely
reporting an incident to police was dropped after she completed a
psycho-education and therapy program on racial equity.[19] In the
case of Walker, both men who harassed her got away with their
behaviors, and the airport security officer was not reprimanded for
his racially insensitive remark.

Amy Cooper and the three men in Walker's incidents also
violated the central theme of CST, which is to respect the dignity
of the human person. Cooper's decision to weaponize her White
fragility is reminiscent of the long tradition of brutality against
Blacks and the anti-Black racism that was punctuated by Carolyn
Bryant who thought the fourteen-year-old Emmett Till might have
whistled at her in her store. For his alleged flirting with a White
woman, her husband, Roy Bryant, and his brother-in-law, J. W.
Milan, kidnapped and brutally murdered Till, dumping his body
into the Tallahatchie River.[20] Cooper's decision to play the race
card in her reporting to the police not only endangered Christian
Cooper but tapped into a long tradition of African Americans
being treated as less than human.

In Walker's incidents, the two men who ridiculed her demonstrated a lack of respect for her dignity as a human being. By
mocking Walker, the older man dehumanized her as an object
of ridicule. The younger man did this by assuming Walker was a

---

[19]   Ryan W. Miller, "Charges Dismissed against Amy Cooper, White
Woman Who Called 911 on Black Bird-Watcher," *Yahoo Money*, Yahoo.com,
February 16, 2021.

[20]   Both Bryant and Milan were acquitted by the all-White and all-male
jury. This brazen acquittal took place a few months before the Montgomery
Bus Boycott, which helped to ignite the Black freedom struggle of the 1950s
and 1960s. See Library of Congress: Civil Rights History Project, "The Murder
of Emmett Till," https://www.loc.gov/collections/civil-rights-history-project/
articles-and-essays/murder-of-emmett-till/.

foreigner who could not speak English. Even after she replied to his query in "perfect" English, he derided her with a fabricated Asian language. The pastoral response, *Encountering Christ in Harmony*, captures this: "For many Asian and Pacific Catholics, the reality of being linguistically or physically different from the larger US population is a constant reminder of their marginalized status. No matter the degree to which they integrate into mainstream culture, racial presumptions may continue to affect them."[21] This dehumanizing treatment of making fun of the manner of speech of Asian Americans or the way they look (e.g., pulling one's eyes back) goes back to the beginning of Chinese immigration to the United States. They were ridiculed for their outward physical appearance as well as for their speech, culture, and social practices. As their number increased over the years, the idea that they were unassimilable to the American way of life emerged along with the nativist fear that they would outnumber Whites in California.

In the case of Christopher Cooper, it was a White person who behaved in a racist manner. In the incident with Amara Walker, at least one of the three men, the first who mocked Walker, was a person of color who, according to Walker, appeared to be a South Asian man. Amy Cooper's behavior was rooted in White privilege and racism, but the South Asian man who verbally assaulted Walker was comfortable enough in his own privilege to utter a racial slur toward her, despite being a person of color himself. While he was not White, that does not take away the sting of his vile action. This raises the long-standing question regarding whether a person of color can be racist. If so, was Tou Thao, the other Minneapolis police officer present during the murder of George Floyd, complicit in the murder of Floyd? Was he complicit in White supremacy?

---

[21] US Conference of Catholic Bishops, *Encountering Christ in Harmony: A Pastoral Response to Our Asian and Pacific Island Brothers and Sisters* (Washington, DC: USCCB, 2018), 18.

Racism as "Powerless Defense"

Toward the end of her interview, Walker added that she received "a bit of flack" on social media after revealing that it was a man of color who uttered a racist slur at her. She added that "there is a misconception out there that only White people are racist or you can't be racist if you're a minority." This misconception can be traced to a reactionary history of the late 1960s when Whites, who were opposed to the advances of the Civil Rights Movement, declared antiracist policies enacted during that period as racist. In response, African Americans in subsequent decades defended themselves against the charges of these "racist Whites" by saying, "Black people can't be racist, because Black people don't have power."[22]

Over time, racism as a political category equated with power became so popular that it has been coined into a simple formula: "racism is prejudice plus power." Joseph Barndt, a Lutheran pastor and antiracism trainer, has promoted this formula in his writings and ministry. Barndt argues that people of color cannot be racist because only White people have the power to enforce their prejudices.[23] Then, in *Understanding and Dismantling Racism*, Barndt clarifies this further by emphasizing that by power he meant institutional and systemic power: "racism is racial prejudice plus the misuse of power by systems and institutions."[24]

Ibram X. Kendi, who wrote the bestseller *How to Be an Antiracist*, calls this sort of understanding of racism the "powerless defense." For Kendi, the powerless defense is a racist idea because it prevents Blacks and other people of color from seeing that they can be racist because power is not something that one group exclusively

---

[22] Ibram X. Kendi, *How to Be an Antiracist* (New York: One World, 2019), 140.

[23] Joseph Barndt, *Dismantling Racism: The Continuing Challenge to White America* (Minneapolis: Augsburg Fortress, 1991), 35.

[24] Joseph Barndt, *Understanding and Dismantling Racism: The Twenty-First-Century Challenge to White America* (Minneapolis: Fortress Press, 2007), 59.

possesses and others do not. Because people of color have some real or perceived power, they can be racist toward their own race or another minoritized group or those who in their view lack power. Indeed, the powerless defense can protect Black racists: Kendi offers an example of the role that Ken Blackwell, Ohio's Black secretary of state, played in the 2004 presidential election in which George W. Bush narrowly won reelection. Among other tactics he employed, Blackwell falsely told former prisoners that they could not vote; allocated fewer voting machines to heavily Democratic cities, which means Black voters on the average had to wait in line eighteen minutes longer than Whites to vote; and accepted voter-registration forms only on an expensive eighty-pound stock paper, to limit the number of qualified Black voters. The powerless defense enabled Blackwell to get away with Black-on-Black racism as he used his power to suppress Black votes.[25]

To be sure, even before Kendi's book, the formula "racism equal prejudice plus power" had been called into question by Michael Omi, Howard Winant, Charles Ridley, and many others. In their 1994 landmark work, *Racial Formation in the United States*, Omi and Winant noted that they could not find empirical evidence to support the argument that only White people can be racist because power is exclusively in the hands of White folks. For them, power cannot be reified as a thing that some possess and others do not.[26] Kendi's powerless defense makes it clear that persons of color can deceive themselves into thinking that they cannot be racist, which according to Kendi is impossible because we all have enough power to be either racist or antiracist. The question of the power-less defense is also seen in the aforementioned Tou Thao, a Hmong American and the former Minneapolis police officer who stood

---

[25] Kendi, *How to Be an Antiracist*, 142–43.

[26] Michael Omi and Howard Winant, *Racial Formation in the United States: From the 1960s to the 1990s* (New York: Routledge, 1994).

guard as his partner, Derek Chauvin, pressed his knee on George Floyd's neck in broad daylight for everyone to witness a modern-day lynching.

In a brazen display of the normalization of police brutality by his partner, Thao exhibited the powerless defense by standing impassively even as onlookers pleaded with him to intervene. By remaining indifferent when his intervention could possibly have made a difference, Thao was complicit in the murder of Floyd and with police brutality. But was Thao complicit with White supremacy? This is not an easy question to answer as the action, or rather inaction, of Tou Thao presents a complicated case.

Given his own 2017 police brutality lawsuit and the six complaints of police misconduct against him, one could argue that as a police officer, Thao was not powerless and this makes him complicit with, or an instrument of, White supremacy. On the other hand, Thao belongs to a Hmong refugee community that resettled in an impoverished neighborhood in Minneapolis. They brought with them a complex intergenerational trauma from their war-torn country of Laos. Unlike the educated Asian immigrants who came to the United States after 1965, Hmong refugees were destitute and uneducated when they resettled in their adopted land. In 2015, the poverty rate of Hmong Americans (28.3 percent) was higher than that of native-born Blacks (24.1 percent), and an alarming 45.3 percent of Hmong Americans had no formal education and only 27 percent had a high school diploma. Coming from such a disproportionately poor community with a shocking high school drop-out rate, it would be hard to argue that Thao benefits from White supremacy or White privilege. As a police officer, however, Thao was not without power. By remaining silent in the midst of adversity, apathetic in moments when action was unequivocally required, Thao was complicit in anti-Blackness. This has led many Asian Americans to interrogate the racialized frameworks they grew up in and has encouraged widespread initiatives to confront anti-Blackness within the Asian American community.

At the individual level, people of color can be racist because they are not completely powerless today. When Walker mentioned that one of her attackers was non-White, her statement was met with strong disagreement by some, many of whom were most likely people of color, who thought of racism as something that only White people could embody. The fact that they can maintain their powerless defense by pushing back on Walker's account reveals that they are not powerless. Moreover, by providing knee-jerk reactions (no evidence) to Walker's post, they were in effect denying her experience and thereby reinforcing the danger of the model minority myth that Asian Americans do not experience racism and discrimination in their everyday life.

The bishops' document *Encountering Christ in Harmony* alludes to how the model minority myth makes racism and discrimination against Asian Americans invisible and how this myth has contributed to the exclusion of Asian Americans and Pacific Islanders (AAPI) in the politics of US racial discourses.[27] In a country in which racial discourse is understood primarily in terms of the Black/White binary, racism and discrimination experienced by Asian Americans, who are seen as model minorities, are often overlooked and ignored. Consequently, AAPI have been consistently excluded in regional and national discussions about race/racism. The model minority myth has also normalized the lie that Asian Americans do not suffer from racism. The reality is that including AAPI in the United States in racial discourses is indispensable to the formation of an antiracist society.

For weeks after the uptick of anti-Asian hate crimes in January 2021, the mainstream media did not report them until they were

---

[27] US Conference of Catholic Bishops, *Encountering Christ in Harmony*, 19–20.

outdone by the number of bystander videos on anti-Asian hate violence posted on social media. Amanda Nguyen, a civil rights activist who was nominated for a Nobel Peace Prize for her work in advocating for sexual assault survivors, challenged the media in February 2021: "How many more people need to be killed in order for the news outlets, especially mainstream ones, to think that we're worthy of a story?"[28]

Anti-Asian xenophobia received a national spotlight during the first week of his presidency when Joe Biden signed an executive order directing federal agencies to combat xenophobia against the AAPI community. After the Atlanta massacre, President Biden redirected $49.5 million of pandemic funds for community-based services for survivors of domestic violence and sexual assault as well as a new task force dedicated to countering xenophobia against Asian Americans in health care.

Claire Jean Kim, professor of political science at the University of California, Irvine, points out that racial triangulation occurs when the dominant group pits Asian Americans against African Americans on cultural and/or racial grounds. While the model minority myth privileges Asian Americans above Blacks in the American racial order, the dominant group also constructs Asian Americans as perpetual foreigners who are too different racially and culturally to be assimilated. Racial triangulation, therefore, consists of these simultaneous, linked processes: the valorization of Asian Americans over Blacks and the ostracization of Asian Americans from the body politics and civic membership.[29] Furthermore, the privileges granted by the model minority status to Asian Americans are conditional and can be taken away at any moment—as during the pandemic when Asian Americans were equated with a virus.

---

[28] Cady Lang, "Hate Crimes against Asian Americans Are on the Rise: Many Say More Policing Isn't the Answer," *TIME*, February 18, 2021.

[29] Claire Jean Kim, "Racial Triangulation," *Politics and Society* 27 (1999): 107.

The conditional privilege and the stigma of enduring outsiders have left Asian Americans quite vulnerable to cycles of aggression from the poor and working-class Americans of all races and ethnicities during times of economic downturn and the threat of a pandemic.

Asian Americans in Danger

As we have mentioned, since the start of 2021, there has been a disturbing trend of violent crimes involving physical assaults on people of Asian descent across the United States. The Center for the Study of Hate and Extremism at the California State University at San Bernardino reports that hate crimes in 2020 were down 7 percent nationally but anti-Asian hate crimes soared to 149 percent in major cities across the United States and, in Sacramento and New York City, skyrocketed to 700 percent and 833 percent.[30] In fact, the "Review of National Anti-Asian Hate Incident Reporting/Data Collection over 2019–2021" reveals that the spike in anti-Asian hate crimes in the above two cities constitutes only 14 percent of all the hate crimes in Sacramento and 11 percent of all reported hate crimes in New York City.

After examining nine sources and four different types of data, including official government crime and law enforcement statistics, community-based reporting systems, such as Stop AAPI Hate, survey data from AAPI Data/Survey Monkey, Pew and Civis Analytics, and media coverage analysis, professor of Asian American studies at the University of Maryland Janelle Wong found that contrary to the prevailing narrative circulated in the media about perpetrators and victims, "more than three-quarters of offenders

---

[30] Center for the Study of Hate and Extremism, "Report to the Nation: Anti-Asian Prejudice & Hate Crime," final draft as of April 28, 2021, page 4, https://www.csusb.edu/sites/default/files/Report%20to%20the%20 Nation%20-%20Anti-Asian%20Hate%202020%20Final%20Draft%20-%20 As%20of%20Apr%2030%202021%206%20PM%20corrected.pdf.

of anti-Asian hate crimes and incidents, from both before and during the pandemic, have been White." Consequently, the media coverage that emphasizes Black-on-Asian hate crimes and incidents can have "long-term consequences for racial solidarity."[31] It threatens to inflame tensions between Black and Asian Americans that have historically been pitted against each other.

Recognizing some notable nuances in anti-Asian incident reporting by various agencies, Wong offers several takeaways from her research roundup. First, "verbal harassment" and "shunning" constitute the vast majority of reported hate incidents. Second, although anti-Asian hate crimes and incidents increased after 2019, they made up about 7 percent of all hate crimes reported in 2020. Even after considering the dramatic increases from 2019 to 2020 in anti-Asian hate crimes in New York City (three to twenty-eight, or an increase of 833 percent) and the city of Sacramento (one to eight, or an increase of 700 percent), the reported anti-Asian hate crimes in New York (11 percent) and Sacramento (14 percent) were lower than the percentage of the Asian American population in New York City (14.5 percent)[32] and Sacramento (20.1).[33]

Third, Black Americans are still the most targeted racial group in the United States. The official 2019 law enforcement statistics show that reported hate crimes were motivated by 58 percent anti-Black bias, 14 percent anti-Latino bias, and 4 percent anti-Asian bias.[34]

Fourth, hate crimes reported to law enforcement and hate

---

[31] Tammy Yam, "Viral Images Show People of Color as Anti-Asian Perpetrators: That Misses the Big Picture," *NBC News*, June 15, 2021.

[32] "Report to the Nation: Anti-Asian Prejudice & Hate Crime," final draft as of April 28, 2021, page 4.

[33] Ibid.

[34] Janelle Wong, "Beyond the Headlines: Review of National Anti-Asian Hate Incident Reporting," June 7, 2021, https://docs.google.com/document/d/19llMUCDHX-hLKru-cnDCq0BirlpNgF07W3f-q0J0ko4/edit.

incidents reported by community-based reporting sites take place predominantly in commercial businesses, public streets, and transit.

Fifth, younger Asian Americans are more inclined than older Asian Americans to report hate incidents to community-based reporting agencies.

Sixth, while all racial groups are uncomfortable reporting a hate crime to law enforcement, Asian Americans are the least at ease to do so.

Seventh, different sources reveal different patterns of reporting with regard to gender, with some sources showing more women reporting anti-Asian hate incidents than men, and other sources showing men were more likely to report than women.

And eighth, the vast majority (75 percent of offenders) of anti-Asian hate crimes and hate incidents have been people of White ancestry.[35]

In summary, while the media coverage of anti-Asian hate crimes tends to focus on violent attacks of Asian Americans by Black and other Americans of color, in reality, anti-Black hate crime represents the vast majority of hate crimes in the United States, and anti-Asian hate incidents make up only 7 percent of all the reported hate crimes in 2020. And White offenders were responsible for 75 percent of anti-Asian hate crimes and incidents in 2021.[36]

Confronting White Supremacy

Prior to the pandemic, anti-Asian hate crimes and incidents against AAPI communities were often dismissed by the American public, and racism experienced by AAPI was often ignored or excluded in the wider racial discourses at local, regional, and national levels. This was due in part to the depiction of Asian Americans as the model

---

[35] Ibid.
[36] Ibid.

minority. During the pandemic, however, there has been a sudden increase in articles and media representations depicting Asians as victims of Black-on-Asian crimes. But because there is a surge of anti-Asian hate crime and violence, there is also disagreement or confusion about whether White supremacy is at the roots of anti-Asian hatred and violence.

Becket Adams, in his April 13, 2021, opinion referred to the 2021 data compiled by Dr. Yan Zhang and colleagues, which corroborate Wong's "Review of National Anti-Asian Hate Incident Reporting," and showed that while 75 percent of transgressors in anti-Asian hate crimes are White, "the proportion of offenders in violent anti-Asian hate crimes are more likely to be non-white."[37] Adams argued that given that about 25 percent of the total number of anti-Asian attacks were committed by non-White offenders, it seems reasonable to conclude that anti-Asian racism goes deeper than White supremacy. He concluded his argument by noting, "It would be false to say people of color are responsible for all anti-Asian attacks" and "are the primary offenders. It is equally wrong, however, to assert white supremacy is at the root of everything insofar as anti-Asian bigotry is concerned."[38] It may be easy to dismiss Adams's assessment as a conservative's attempt to pit Asian and African Americans, but he was reflecting an honest assessment of many Whites who questioned how White supremacy is at the root of everything when the primary offenders of violent anti-Asian attacks are non-White offenders.

Asian American scholars, community organizers, and activists have maintained that the source of both anti-Asian racism and anti-Black racism is White supremacy. By White supremacy, they

---

[37] Yan Zhang et al. "Hate Crimes against Asian Americans," *American Journal of Criminal Justice: AJCJ* (2021): 1–21.

[38] Becket Adams, "MSNBC Blames Anti-Asian Crimes on White Supremacy, but the Data Shows There's More to the Story," *Washington Examiner*, April 13, 2021.

are referring not to racist terrorist groups like the Ku Klux Klan, neo-Nazis, or White nationalism, but rather the ideology of White supremacy that has permeated this nation since its foundation— constructing Asian Americans as immutably alien (perpetual foreigner stereotype) and as the model minority in relation to other people of color. White supremacy is reflective of ongoing systemic racism that has enabled the dehumanization of Chinese, Chinese Americans, and other Asian Americans who look Chinese by equating all with the novel coronavirus. This is the same White supremacy that enabled an economic system of slavery that brought over 400,000 Africans as slaves to the United States across generations, which means millions of African Americans were enslaved, followed by institutional degradation, Jim Crow laws, segregation, police brutality, and other forms of anti-Blackness.

Jennifer Ho, president of the Association for Asian American Studies and critical race scholar, focuses on this when she notes: "The dehumanization of Asian people by U.S. society is driven by White supremacy and not by any Black person who may or may not hate Asians."[39] This sounds like Black people cannot dehumanize Asian people. But this is not what Ho is saying. Her point is that the ideology of White supremacy pervades the environment in which we live and operate. As Ho writes, "The white supremacy I'm talking about is in the air we breathe and the water we drink. There is simply no escaping the reach of white supremacy."[40] In other words, White supremacy influences everything that we (both Whites and non-Whites) do.

However, we are not mere puppets, passively conforming to the prescription of the ideology even though we are influenced by it. We are responsible for our own actions. We are not without

---

[39] Jennifer Ho, "White Supremacy Is the Root of All Race-Related Violence in the US," *The Conversation*, April 8, 2021.

[40] Jennifer Ho, "Anti-Asian Racism, Black Lives Matter, and COVID-19," *Japan Forum* 33, no. 1 (2020): 148–59.

agency. If a person of color chooses to dehumanize an Asian person as the Other by uttering racial slurs or assaulting them, then the person is guilty of either a hate incident or a hate crime. One does not need to be White to engage in White supremacist behavior. There are members within all communities of color who have internalized White supremacist ideas and bigotry to the extent that some expressed them, sometimes in both words and deeds, without giving it a second thought. This demonstrates the power and pervasiveness of White supremacy as it influences not only our values and thought forms but also our instinctual responses. It shows up when people of color, consciously or unconsciously, choose to utter ethnic slurs or use negative stereotypes against each other. At a deeper level, it shows up when members of the Asian American community advocate for a right-wing political agenda that will roll back the advances of the race conscious reform of the Civil Rights Era, or when members of the Black community are preoccupied with their own suffering to the degree that it blinds them to their own unconscious biases, prejudices, or racism they might have regarding others.

In his discussion of the powerless defense, Kendi reminds us that "Black people can be racist because Black people do have power, even if limited."[41] At the individual level, all of us, irrespective of our race, gender, and other belongings, can be racist. At the collective level, no community is powerless enough to say that it does not have the power to commit racism. No person or group is immune. None of us is perfect, either individually or collectively. We are often blind to stereotypes we have been accustomed to and hold unconscious biases and prejudices in our psyches. It is in this spirit of honest assessment that we will look at some of the horrific crimes in which Asian American victims were either seriously injured or killed during the first four months of 2021

---

[41] Kendi, *How to Be an Anti-Racist,* 142.

and the first three months of 2022. This will also help us better understand some common characteristics exhibited in these violent crimes and demonstrate the difficulty of declaring a violent crime as a hate crime in the court of law. There were many horrific crimes committed against Asian Americans during the first four months of 2021 and 2022, but I will mention eleven of them and examine only three of them at some depth.

On January 28, Vicha Ratanapakdee, an eighty-four-year-old Thai American man died from injuries sustained after Antoine Watson, a nineteen-year-old Black teenager, sprinted toward the victim and violently shoved him, knocking him to the ground, and afterward, showed no remorse for what he had done.[42] The public defender representing Watson declared that the suspect had a mental health issue and that this was a crime of opportunity.[43]

On February 3, Noel Quintana, a sixty-one-year-old Filipino American, a religious man, boarded the subway in New York City on his way to work. He was praying the rosary on a crowded train when a deranged Black man boarded at Bedford Station, targeted him at random, and slashed him across the face with a box cutter. Quintana was rushed to the hospital where he received more than one hundred stiches. In his interview with Eyewitness News ABC7, Quintana said, "I was scared because I thought I was gonna to die and nobody helped me."[44]

On February 26, a thirty-six-year-old Asian American man was stabbed with an eight-inch knife in the back while walking home in New York City's Chinatown. Salman Muflihi, a twenty-three-year-

---

[42] Michael Barba, "Judge Orders Detention for Teen Held in Fatal Attack," *San Francisco Examiner*, February 8, 2021.

[43] Saumya Dixit, "Who Is Antoine Watson? SF Teen Who Killed 84-Year-Old Man by Shoving Him to Pavement Pleads Not Guilty," *Media Entertainment Arts Worldwide*, February 9, 2021.

[44] Lindsay Wang, "Elderly FilAm Attacked with Knife in NYC Metro, No One Helped," *AsAm News*, February 9, 2021.

old Arab American, was charged with second-degree attempted murder. Muflihi allegedly told detectives that "I stabbed that guy. If he dies, he dies. I don't give a f---."[45] Although Muflihi stated that he "didn't like the way [the victim] looked at him," the authorities did not consider this a hate crime because he may have never actually seen the victim's face as he stabbed him from behind.[46]

On March 15, Filipino–Chinese Danny Yu Chang, a fifty-nine-year-old travel agent, was walking through San Francisco's financial district when an assailant punched his head from behind and knocked him unconscious to the ground. The assailant must have continued punching Yu Chang's face as he lay on the ground since he suffered from a fractured face and serious eye injuries. In his interview, the victim said, "They didn't rob me so I think it's a hate crime." Sadly, the Latino suspect, Jorge Devis-Milton, who also stabbed a sixty-four-year-old White man an hour before attacking Chang, will not be charged with a hate crime unless he made a racist remark and someone was witness to it.[47]

On March 16, Robert Aaron Long, a twenty-one-year-old White assailant, went on a shooting spree and murdered eight people, six of whom were Asian women, at three spas in greater Atlanta. While Long claimed that the shooting was not racially motivated and that he had sexual addiction problems, racism experienced by Asian American women often has sexual overtones with misogyny intertwined with it. This case is still under investigation.[48]

On March 17, Xiao Zhen Xie, a seventy-five-year-old elderly

---

[45] Aaron Katersky, Emily Shapiro, and Meredith Deliso, "Asian Man Stabbed in Chinatown, Suspect Charged with Attempted Murder," *ABC News*, February 27, 2021.

[46] Phil Helsel, "Suspect Faces Hate Crime Charges in Stabbing of Asian Man in New York City," *NBC News*, February 26, 2021.

[47] "UPDATE: SF Police Link Suspect in Attack that Almost Blinded Asian Man to Brutal Mission District Stabbing," CBS San Francisco, March 17, 2021.

[48] "Atlanta Shootings: Suspect Charged with Murder as Victims Identified," BBC News, March 18, 2021.

Asian woman, turned the tables on her attacker by picking up a
stick and fighting back after being assaulted by Steven Jenkins, a
thirty-nine-year-old White assailant who was homeless at the
time.[49] The same attacker also assaulted an eighty-three-year-old
Asian man that same day. The public defender is arguing that this
was not a hate crime as he shared a new surveillance video that
shows that Jenkins himself was a victim of over forty blows from
multiple people before stumbling near Xie and taking a swing
at her. The question remains whether he was cognizant when he
assaulted Xie and eighty-three-year-old Ngoc Pham, and the two
elderly Asian persons he attacked were not also his attackers.[50]

On March 29, a vicious attack took place on a Midtown
Manhattan sidewalk. On her way to church, a sixty-five-year-old
Filipina was kicked unprovoked by Brandon Elliot, a thirty-eight-
year-old burly Black man who was on lifetime parole after being
convicted of fatally stabbing his mother in 2002. As the elderly
Filipina, Vilma Kari, lay stunned on the sidewalk after receiving
Elliot's kick to her stomach, he uttered racial slurs as he walked
over her and stomped on her head three times.[51] Of all the violent
crimes mentioned above, this is the only one that has been officially
declared a hate crime at the time of this writing.

On April 15, 2021, during the week when Sikhs were celebrating Vaisakhi, which marks the start of the Punjabi New Year,
and celebrating the year 1699 when Sikhism was born as a collective faith, four Sikhs were among the eight people killed in the
mass shooting at a FedEx warehouse in Indianapolis. The shooter,

---

[49] Cheryl Teh, "An Elderly Asian Woman Fought Back against a Man
Who Attacked Her, and a Video Appears to Show Him Bloodied on a
Stretcher," *Yahoo News*, Yahoo.com, March 18, 2021.

[50] Andre Torrez, "SF Defender Says Client's Actions Weren't Race Based,
Shares Revealing Video," *Fox KTVU*, April 9, 2021.

[51] Nicole Hong, Juliana Kim, et al., "Brutal Attack on Filipino Woman
Sparks Outrage: 'Everybody Is on Edge,'" *New York Times*, March 30, 2021.

Brandon Scott Hole, a nineteen-year-old White suspect, began randomly firing at people in the parking lot of the FedEx facility, killing four, before entering the building, murdering four more, and then turning the gun on himself.[52]

And in 2022, there was a string of vicious attacks against Asian American women. On January 15, a forty-year-old Michelle Go was shoved in front of an oncoming train by Simon Martial, a sixty-one-year-old homeless ex-convict with a history of living with a mental illness.[53]

On February 13, thirty-five-year-old Christina Yuna Lee entered her apartment building as a twenty-five-year-old homeless man, Assamad Nash, followed her to her apartment and savagely stabbed her dozens of times to her death.[54]

On March 15, a sixty-seven-year-old Filipina was trying to open the door to enter the lobby of the building where she resides when a forty-two-year-old homeless man, Tammel Esco, punched her head from behind and continued punching her more than 125 times and stomped on her seven times while uttering racist profanities.[55] Of all the crimes mentioned above, only those committed by Brandon Elliot and Tammel Esco have been officially declared as hate crimes so far.

All of these examples tell us that counting the number of hate crimes does not inform us about the gravity or severity of each of them. Should a shooting spree of a lone White gunman, murdering

---

[52] Casey Smith and Rick Callahan, "Four Sikhs Among Victims of Indianapolis Fedex Mass Shooting: The Shooter's Motives Remain Unknown," *Denver Post*, April 17, 2021.

[53] Nicole Chavez, "Michelle Go's Death Hasn't Been Labeled as a Hate Crime but Adds to the Fear Asian Americans Feel," CNN.com, January 20, 2022.

[54] Amara Walker, "I Can't Stop Thinking That I Could Have Been Christina Yuna Lee," CNN.com, February 28, 2022.

[55] Liam Reilly, "Asian Woman Stomped on and Punched More than 125 Times after Being Called Racial Slur, Police Say," CNN.com, March 15, 2022.

eight people, six of whom were Asian women, be counted in the same way as an offender of color throwing a sucker punch at an Asian person? While there were more non-White offenders involved in anti-Asian violent crimes in the first four months of 2021, two Whites killed sixteen people, ten of whom were Asian Americans. Unfortunately, we need to have a separate mass murder category in the collection and reporting of this data.

Many in the Asian American community and perhaps those who saw the surveillance videos of these crimes, would consider all of the above assaults to be hate crimes. In a court of law, however, one has to prove beyond a reasonable doubt that the motive of the person committing a violent crime was based on "perceived or actual race, color, religion, national origin, sexual orientation, gender, gender identity, or disability."[56] For example, Elliot was charged with a hate crime in part because he made anti-Asian remarks during the assault and told her "you don't belong here." Tammel Esco was charged with a hate crime because his racist profanities made it explicit he was attacking an elderly Filipina because of her race.

Another example of a hate crime that does not involve a vicious assault was a man who punched an Asian American worker in the face in a Manhattan 7-Eleven store on April 4, 2021, which was investigated as a hate crime because the suspect yelled, "You Chinese motherf---er!" before he punched the worker.[57] However, the nineteen-year-old Watson who violently barreled into Ratanapakdee is not charged with a hate crime because he did not say anything that would incriminate himself, even though

---

[56] "What Is a Hate Crime?" *U.S. Department of Justice*, https://www.justice.gov/hatecrimes/learn-about-hate-crimes. According to the US Department of Justice, a hate crime consists of a violent crime and a motivation for committing the crime based on bias.

[57] Tina Moore and Jorge Fitz-Gibbon, "Manhattan 7-Eleven Worker Punched, Called Chinese 'motherf-er,'" *New York Post*, April 4, 2021.

his action killed a man. It seems that actions do not always speak louder than words in the court of law. To be charged with a hate crime, the suspect must utter a racial slur or have a history of racist behavior. To say an incident is not a hate crime means within a narrow limit of the law, it could not be determined beyond a reasonable doubt that the perpetrator had a motivation to commit a crime based on bias.

However, this does not mean the incident was without hate or racism. The legal definition of a hate crime, for example, may not take into account the ways in which Asian Americans are racially perceived in American history and the entertainment industry. The Atlanta massacre is a good example that involves the intersection of race, gender (the perception of Asian women as sex objects), and violence (US involvement in wars in Asia)—even though it is currently not investigated as a hate crime.

In the Atlanta-area spa shootings, the suspect, Robert Long, son of a Baptist pastor, claimed that his actions were not racially motivated and that he had a "sexual addiction" problem. Although at the time of this writing, it was too early for authorities to declare these shootings a hate crime, it was clear to many Asian Americans that Long went into Asian massage parlors to target members of their community. This tragic murder of six Asian women brought to the surface the notion of gendered racism, the idea that Asian women experience racism differently from Asian men.

Racism experienced by Asian and Asian American women often has a sexual overtone. According to Sung Yeon Choimorrow, director of National Asian Pacific American Women's Forum, hypersexualization of Asian women's bodies can be traced back to the nineteenth century when Chinese women who managed to come to the United States were assumed to be prostitutes. Fast forward about a hundred years later, and during the Vietnam War, Asian women were hypersexualized and commodified for the pleasure of the US soldiers during their rest and recreation in Thailand or the Philippines. These fantasies and fetishes were brought back to the states, and they continue to be objectified in Hollywood and popular culture.[58] The 2018 report of a survey conducted by the American Psychological Association asserts that the depiction of Asian women as "quiet and invisible, or as sexual objects" has endured in the America media and popular culture.[59] For many, the hypersexualization of Asian women and misogyny are deeply intertwined and have often led to violence. For them, the Atlanta massacre was not simply a "sexual addiction" problem of a White male suspect, but rather a stark reminder of how gendered racism has dehumanized the bodies of six Asian women who died: Soon Chung Park, Suncha Kim, Yong Ae Yue, Delaina Ashley Yaun, Xiaojie Tan, and Daoyou Feng.

In a March 16, 2021, interview with *Asian America* magazine, Russell Jeung, professor of Asian American Studies at San Francisco State University and cofounder of Stop AAPI Hate, spoke of "a distinction between this particular violence [perpetuated by suspects], most of which has not been found to be explicitly racially motivated, and the racism those in the community have been facing due to the problematic link between the virus and Asian Americans." This distinction is important to keep in mind to avoid the criminalization of the entire group of people. Kimmy Yam, author of the same article, also interviewed Karthick Ramakrishnan, founder and director of the demographic data and policy research nonprofit AAPI Data, who warns against a simplistic understanding of anti-Asian violence without taking into consideration "a confluence of factors, including the effects of poverty and

---

[58] Sung Yeon Choimorrow, "A Discussion on Hypersexualization as a Form of Racism against Asian American Women," March 18, 2021, https://www.youtube.com/watch?v=J7HVwblE21w.

[59] Shruti Mukkamala and Karen L. Suyemoto, "From Exotic to Invisible: Asian American Women's Experience of Discrimination," *American Psychological Association*, July 26, 2018.

financial struggle exacerbated by the pandemic, as well as opportunity, could have played into it."[60]

Poverty and lack of opportunities for young people in inner
cities are associated with the larger institutional and structural
problems in our society. In his study of low employment among
Black men, Harry J. Holzer, John LaFarge Professor of Public
Policy at Georgetown University, demonstrates that Black men
have the highest unemployment rate of any racial group, and the
lowest labor force participation among men. This is due to the
greater experience of discrimination, as well as lower education and
work experience, which are major determining factors of employment and earnings in the United States.[61]

One of the commonalities among the perpetrators of the
sort of violent crimes discussed above is mental health issues. You
may have noticed this common thread in my accounting of the
incidents. Having said this, we have to be careful not to stigma-
tize people living with mental health problems. In her analysis of
429 crimes committed by 143 offenders, Dr. Jillian Peterson, a
psychology professor at Normandie Community College, found
that a vast majority of people with mental health problems are
not violent people or dangerous criminals. Most offenders did not
show a pattern of crime related to symptoms of mental illness over
their lifetimes.[62] Recent studies on the link between mental illness
and violent acts corroborates Dr. Peterson's 2014 finding that when
people with serious mental illness commit violent acts or crimes,
other factors such as substance abuse, poverty, and homelessness,
as well as having been abused as a child, or environmental factors,

---

[60] Kimmy Yam, "There Were 3,800 Anti-Asian Racist Incidents, Mostly
against Women in Past Year," *NBC News*, March 16, 2021.

[61] Harry J. Holzer, "Why Are Employment Rates so Low among Black
Men?" *Brookings*, March 1, 2021.

[62] Jillian Peterson, "Mental Illness not usually linked to crime, research
finds," *American Psychological Association*, April 15, 2014.

such as living in a high-crime neighborhood, are often at play.[63] This is one of the areas that both Black and Asian Americans can work together on as both communities are faced with inadequate resources to deal with mental health problems within their respective communities.

The media also influences how the public sees these violent crimes as they tend to accentuate Black-on-Asian crimes that fit into the narrative of the model minority myth that continues to pit the two communities against each other. Because media rarely mentions the race of the assailant or include a photo of the attacker in their reporting, internet comments are filled with the assumption about "the usual suspect"—that is, Black assailant. This sort of assumption, in addition to ample video footage of Black men attacking Asians on social media, augments the idea of Black criminality and can lead to the overreliance on law enforcement and the criminal justice system to address anti-Asian violence. In other words, the fear is that depicting Blacks as villains can lead to more police presence, which then contributes to the criminalization of African Americans. This sentiment is echoed by community organizers and activists who caution against tougher policing, which can lead to discriminatory policing that targets Black and Brown bodies at disproportionate rates.

However, not everyone in the Asian American community is convinced that expanding policing is a bad thing. Small shop owners in Chinatown plead for more police presence, especially during the Chinese New Year. In general, store owners and senior citizens in Chinatown are in favor of greater police protection and presence. In one such community, when meetings were led by progressives, some Asian Americans were offended that instead of talking about the safety and security of the elderly in their commu-

---

[63] Tori DeAngelis, "Mental illness and violence: Debunking myths, addressing realities," *American Psychological Association*, April 1, 2021.

nity, discussions of Black men attacking Asian elderly were used as teachable moments to discuss anti-Black racism.[64] Chris Kwok, board member of the Asian American Bar Association, echoed this view succinctly when he said, "I certainly understand the desire not to unfairly criminalize African Americans and Latinos, but I think we also need to have accountability for these attacks."[65]

By accountability he meant, among other things, that if a community is under attack, it has the right to take appropriate actions to protect itself. There is, however, another kind of accountability we need. This is a challenge to call each other's community to accountability, not by passing judgment but by examining each community's unconscious biases and prejudices and changing our behaviors from racist to antiracist.

In his bestseller, Kendi tells us that "the heartbeat of racism is denial and the heartbeat of anti-racism is confession." For Kendi, being a racist or antiracist is not ontological; it's not about who you are. Rather, it's about what you have said and done. Because it is expressed at the behavioral level, we have the capacity to change our behavior from racist to antiracist. To do this, however, we have to admit that we are racist when we have said or done something racist. As noted, Kendi's notion of the powerless defense expresses that anyone from any race or ethnicity can be a racist because no one is completely powerless. A good example of this notion is the heinous crime that took place in front of Hell's Kitchen in midtown Manhattan. Despite the fact that Elliot was on parole and had spent the majority of his life in prison, he demonstrated his power when he centered himself as the insider and shouted, "You don't belong here!" while stomping the head of Kari, a Filipina mother. He assumed he had more power than she by internalizing

---

[64] Vivian Ho and Abené Clayton, "'Black and Asian Unity': Attacks on Elders Spark Reckoning with Racism's Roots," *The Guardian*, February 21, 2021.

[65] Masood Farivar, "Anti-Asian Hate Crime Crossed Racial and Ethnic Lines," *VOA News*, March 24, 2021.

an exclusionary nationalistic idea rooted in White supremacy that Asians cannot be fully American without realizing that he himself was also at the margins of American society.

Anti-Blackness and Colorism

Many first-generation Asian immigrants may not have heard about the model minority myth, much less understood its association with anti-Blackness. Arriving after the Civil Rights Movement, and from countries with limited or no freedom, they saw themselves as outsiders in Black/White tensions that have been going on for centuries. It is understandable that they would want to remain silent and stay out of harm's way. However, after they have acclimated to their new environment and have become naturalized US citizens, they are no longer outsiders even if they are considered as such by many native-born Americans. The more Asian Americans of all generations consciously or unconsciously ascribe to the myth of the model minority that Asian Americans, through sole recourse to their own efforts, are able to pull themselves up out of racism by their own bootstraps, so to speak, the more they buy into the anti-Blackness and the negative stereotypes about Black people.

Since the majority of Asian Americans are foreign born, I will begin with anti-Black racism in Asia. Contemporary African immigration to China is a fairly recent phenomenon resulting from the Belt-and-Road Initiative, a global infrastructure development strategy with direct investments from state-owned and private enterprises in Africa and the inevitable movements of people to and from Africa. There has been a growing presence of Africans in China since 1990, and there are now over 500,000 African and African Americans living in China. This is still a drop in the bucket in a country with more than 1.4 billion people.

In a seemingly homogenous society, where most Chinese have had limited or no contact with Black people, tensions and conflicts are to be expected—especially during a public health crisis. In Guangzhou, where the majority of African immigrants reside, the coronavirus pandemic has led to the scapegoating of Africans as carriers of the virus, leading to a racialized campaign of compulsory testing of Africans for the coronavirus, and reports of racial discrimination against African immigrants in employment, housing, and other sectors.[66] In Japan, Korea, Vietnam, and the Philippines, anti-Black racism is evident in the differential treatment of White-Amerasian children vis-à-vis their Black counterparts.

Because there are very few people of African descent in Asia, "anti-Black" racism,[67] in its broadest understanding, has traditionally been directed mostly to people of a darker skin color, often of South Asian descent, who live and work throughout Southeast Asia. For example, the Black Lives Matter Movement's protests in the United States provided the needed courage for activists in Myanmar (Burma) to openly protest against the use of the disdainful word *kalar* (pronounced "kalah") in reference to individuals from the Indian subcontinent who were seen as outcasts in their own country because of their darker complexion.[68] Thus, even before COVID-19, Rohingya and other Muslim minority groups experienced "anti-Black" racism and were assaulted in Myanmar, India, and Sri Lanka. Indeed, in 2017, Facebook took down posts containing the word *kalar* from Myanmar Facebook users as a way to expel the use of the word to promote racism and hate speech

---

[66] Amanuel Elias, Jehonathan Ben, Fethi Mansouri, and Yin Paradies, "Racism and Nationalism during and beyond the COVID-19 Pandemic," *Ethnic and Racial Studies* 44, no. 5 (2021): 788.

[67] I am not expanding the term *Black*, as understood within the American context, to include people from the Indian subcontinent. I am using the term to imply that anti-Black sentiments among Asian immigrants was influenced in part by how people with darker skin complexion were treated in Asia.

[68] "Why Myanmar Is Rejecting the 'Kalar' Campaign," *Myanmar Mix*, June 15, 2020.

by ultranationalists and religious fundamentalists who attack the Rohingya minority.[69]

Anti-Blackness runs deep in Asia. For example, women in the Indian subcontinent and East Asia are socialized to believe that a light skin complexion is better than a darker one and is the key to success in life and marriage.[70] This appeal for Whiteness has been reinforced by Hollywood's marketing and representations of films with White lead actors and mostly White casts based on the assumption that Black films and actors would not appeal to international audiences, more specifically, the vast market of Asian audiences. Many of these films portrayed Black people in a negative light. And even when they are depicted in a seemingly positive light, film narratives tend to highlight White normativity and/ or superiority.[71] These films become "a vehicle for 'transnational racialization,' inculcating racial hierarchy to those who have not been regularly exposed to black and white people."[72]

So even before migrating to the United States, Asian immigrants and refugees have been exposed to anti-Blackness through American films and other forms of entertainment that are circulated through cultural globalization. This does not help those refugees who are resettled across the country, usually in Black and Brown neighborhoods, with no orientation to the history of their new neighbors or introduction to the leaders of the local community, toward a proper understanding.

---

[69] Juan Cebu, "Facebook Bans Racist Word 'Kalar' in Myanmar, Triggers Collateral Censorship," *Advox*, June 2, 2017.

[70] Leland Ware, "'Color Struck': Intragroup and Cross-racial Color Discrimination," *The Geography of Colorism*, January 2, 2014.

[71] Minjeong Kim and Rachelle J. Brunn-Bevel, "Hollywood's Global Expansion and Racialized Film Industry," *Humanity and Society* 44, no. 1 (2020): 41.

[72] Nadia Kim, *Imperial Citizens: Koreans and Race from Seoul to LA* (Stanford, CA: Stanford University Press, 2008), 12–14.

The Backgrounders' section of *Open Wide Our Hearts*, reminds Catholics that "[a] truly welcoming community does not emerge by chance but is established through the hard work and conviction of local residents, through direct service, sharing experiences, faith, advocacy, and institution building."[73] What is often missing in these resettlement programs is the presence of representatives or leaders of color from the Black or Brown community to welcome and orient newcomers into their neighborhood. People who help refugees resettle in their new neighborhood are usually White pastoral leaders and volunteers who are of tremendous assistance to the refugees but do not live in Black and Brown communities themselves. As a result, the refugees are left to fend for themselves, so to speak, in a formation of silo communities, which reinforces the anti-Black images and stereotypes they have brought with them. Because the refugees are generally resettled in poorer neighborhoods, which are already limited in resources, the federal government should create more jobs and provide resources in communities where refugees are resettled. It should be a "win-win" situation for both the long-time residents of that community and the newly arrived.

For Asian immigrants who settled in White suburbs, anti-Black sentiments and stereotypes also commonly persist as the Asians have limited contact with Black people. This means that unlearning the ways in which anti-Blackness manifests itself in the everyday life of an Asian American is a necessary step toward dismantling anti-Blackness within the Asian American community. For refugees, this unlearning of anti-Blackness would have been a lot easier if space and time were set aside for local representatives or leaders in the respective Black or Brown community to meet

---

[73] US Conference of Catholic Bishops, *Open Wide Our Hearts*, "Racism and Migration in the United States," https://www.usccb.org/issues-and-action/human-life-and-dignity/racism/upload/racism-and-migration.pdf

and welcome them, which would also help to ease their transitions into their new neighborhood. There are many hospitable people in Black and Brown communities. They need to be tapped in the resettlement of refugees from any country, and hospitality is the best avenue for building solidarity.

Deconstructing anti-Blackness is tied to deconstructing colorism, the idea that within non-White races, lighter skin individuals are perceived as more beautiful and receive preferential treatment as well as the establishment of a social hierarchy based on shades of skin tone within and between racialized communities. Colorism is prevalent not only in Asian and Asian American communities but also African American, Latinx, and other communities of color. Colorism divides individuals within communities of color because it allows those who most closely resemble the White standard of beauty or of a near-White appearance to have an easier time gaining social acceptance and reaping the benefits of what our racialized society has to offer.

In Asia, colorism predates colonialism. In India, obsession with Whiteness is deeply entrenched, and a superior lineage claimed by upper caste members can be traced to the belief in Aryan racial supremacy in which light-skinned individuals are considered beautiful and superior, and dark-skinned individuals are rendered as ugly and inferior.[74] In China and Japan, light skinned individuals are associated with people of a higher class as their jobs do not require them to toil in the sun. The saying that light skinned individuals are more beautiful is a common expression in many Asian countries. In her article, "Consuming Lightness," Evelyn Nakano Glenn points out that the association of physical attractiveness with light skin is especially critical for many Asian women

---

[74] Varsha Ayyar and Lalit Khandare, "Mapping Color and Caste Discrimination in Indian Society," in *The Melanin Millennium: Skin Color as 21st Century International Discourse* (New York: Springer, 2013), 80.

and the search for this unchangeable capital "takes the form of using cosmetics or other treatments to change the appearance of one's skin to make it look lighter."[75] Demand for skin lightening creams in the global market was estimated to be 8.6 billion dollars in 2020.[76] In their study, Rondilla and Spickard note that the desire for light skin among Asians has to do with class rather than race.[77] Nevertheless, the preference for lighter skinned individuals reinforces Whiteness and thus contributes to anti-Blackness. This is something that Asian Americans have to reckon with if we are to undo the legacy of anti-Blackness within our communities.

What many immigrants of all races and ethnicity also fail to realize is that our reception by and incorporation into American society would have been more difficult had it not been for generations of African Americans fighting for their rights and self-determination. The African American Civil Rights Movement paved the way for the rights that Asian Americans and other non-African American minorities take for granted today. The passage of the Civil Rights Act of 1964, as well as the Voting Rights Act of 1965, would not have been possible without the Civil Rights Movement that inspired the abolishment of the race-based immigration quota system and replaced it with the Immigration and Nationality Act of 1965. This has enabled many of us to emigrate to the United States, meaning, Asian Americans owe a debt of gratitude to their African American counterparts for the rights they enjoy today. This is something about which many in the immigrant generation and, even in the present generation, may not be fully aware.

---

[75] Evelyn Nakano Glenn, "Consuming Lightness: Segmented Markets and Global Capital in the Skin-Whitening Trade," in *Shades of Difference: Why Skin Color Matters* (Stanford, CA: Stanford University Press, 2009), 166–67.

[76] Ronald Hall, "It's 2021 and Skin Bleaching Is Still a Billion-Dollar Industry," *Mic*, February 22, 2021.

[77] Trina Jones, "The Significance of Skin Color in Asian and Asian American Communities: Initial Reflections," *UC Irvine Law Review* 3 (2013): 1116.

Furthermore, many African American leaders have stood behind Asian Americans in times of need and suffering. Malcolm X was the first prominent African American leader to speak up against the Vietnam War. At the request of Thich Nhat Hanh, Dr. Martin Luther King Jr. denounced the Vietnam War, as well, knowing fully that he would lose some of his supporters for backing a non-Black related cause, even though the war was costing Black lives and resources that could have been used for domestic needs.

In 1982, Jesse Jackson took time from his presidential bid to show support for Asian Americans, seeking justice for Vincent Chin, a Chinese American who was brutally beaten to death with a baseball bat by two unemployed White auto workers that year. Today, Reverend Jackson is working with Dr. Grace Ji-Sun Kim and other religious leaders of the Korean American community to seek peace and reconciliation in the Korean Peninsula.

As anti-Asian hate incidents have surged with COVID-19, many Black leaders have denounced anti-Asian racism and xenophobia. Since African American leaders have stood up for Asian Americans in times of our suffering, and since White supremacy is the common cause for both anti-Asian racism and anti-Black racism, it is time for Asian Americans to stand behind African Americans in their suffering and in the common quest of both Black and Asian Americans to reckon with racial injustice and inequality.

Conclusion and Theological Reflection

To tackle racism, Asian Americans in the 1940s presented themselves as having the right values and cultures to assimilate into mainstream American culture. Similar narratives were put forth by other racial minorities, including African Americans, to resist racism faced by all minoritized groups. However, during clamors for equal rights and self-determination by African Americans in the 1950s and '60s, neoconservatives and political leaders heard only the Asian voices.

To win allies in the Cold War and, later, to reverse the advances of the Civil Rights Movement in the 1960s, they co-opted the narratives put forth by Chinese and Japanese Americans and eventually distorted them into the model minority myth.[78] In doing so, they changed the dynamic of the original Asian Americans' call for respect and acceptance in American society by redirecting the frustration of Black and Brown communities toward Asian Americans, and keeping the dominant group from having to address the structural and systemic factors that have prevented the advancement of Black and Brown Americans. Consequently, the ideology of White supremacy continues to operate by pitting Asian Americans against other people of color and rendering invisible racism and discrimination experienced by people of Asian descent and Pacific Islanders in the United States.

Because of the depiction of Asian Americans as alien Others or people who are seen as foreigners in their own country, a better approach to understanding the racial positioning of Asian Americans is through Ancheta's insider/outsider spectrum, which centers on citizenship rather than the Black/White binary centered on race. This does not mean the Black/White binary has no relevance to Asian Americans. It means that in most instances, the type of racism encountered by Asian Americans is nativist, and positions them as either the model minority or forever foreigner. The status of the model minority or honorary White is conditional and, in times of adversity, can collapse into the forever foreigner. We saw that with Amara Walker who, by all accounts, is an honorary White, yet was treated as a perpetual foreigner by the first two people she encountered at the New Orleans International Airport.

The model minority myth captures the ways in which Asian Americans are racially positioned in both the insider/outsider spec-

---

[78] Emily Wu, *The Color of Success: Asian Americans and the Origin of the Model Minority* (Princeton, NJ: Princeton University Press, 2015), 2.

trum and Black/White binary, as a function of White supremacy and anti-Blackness in the United States. The model minority trope places Asian Americans above African Americans in the Black/White binary. Structurally, this makes Asian Americans more privileged than African Americans. According to Mari Matsuda, professor at the UCLA School of Law, Asian Americans, as a racial middle, have a critical role to play—they can either reinforce White supremacy or dismantle it "if it refuses to be the middle, if it refuses to buy into racial hierarchy, if it refuses to abandon communities of Black and Brown people, choosing instead to form alliances with them."[79] Simply put, forming a coalition with Black, Brown, and White allies is essential for Asian Americans to do their part to dismantle White supremacy.

The function of the model minority myth to obscure anti-Asian racism and to pit Asian Americans with other people of color goes against the meaning of justice articulated in the pastoral letter against racism, namely, the importance of establishing a "right relationship with God, with one another, and with the rest of God's creation."[80] Forming a right relationship with God and with one another is based on Jesus's great commandments, a combination of Deuteronomy 6:5: "Therefore, you shall love the Lord, your God, with all your heart, and with all your soul, and with all your strength," and Leviticus 19:18: "Take no revenge and cherish no grudge against your fellow countrymen. You shall love your neighbor as yourself." This expresses the totality of God's will summed up in loving obedience to God and to neighbors. To love God, we must love all our neighbors, which includes our enemies. The word *enemy* conveys a mental and moral power that makes violence possible, even necessary. When the enemy becomes a

---

[79] Mari Matsuda, "Voices of the Community: We Will Not Be Used," A talk presented at the Asian Law Caucus, Yumpu.com, April 1990.

[80] US Conference of Catholic Bishops, *Open Wide Our Hearts*, 6.

person, when we realize they have feelings, desires, and expectations just as we do, we are less likely to do them harm. In other words, justice is a starting point for dealing with personal, social, and moral issues.

To do justice requires us to examine our lives both individually and collectively in our failures, attempting to "walk humbly with your God" (Mi 6:8). Sin is a personal or corporate failure to walk in the way of God. Such an understanding of sin correlates with theologian Karl Rahner's notion of fundamental option theory, which is used as a corrective to the pre–Vatican II understanding of sin that was considered too act centered, individualistic, and legalistic. For Rahner, a transcendental freedom enables people to orient themselves either toward God or away from God. Sinful acts, which move us away from God, manifest the deeper reality of the transcendental freedom and cannot be equated with acts themselves. However, when we seek to satisfy our deepest longings, there is no way of avoiding the inevitable encounter with God.[81]

Although the bishops' letter *Open Wide Our Hearts* does not cite Rahner's works, it does emphasize that "[r]acist acts are sinful because they violate justice. They reveal a failure to acknowledge the human dignity of the persons offended, to recognize them as the neighbors Christ calls us to love (Mt 22:39)."[82] Racism as a sin is a failure to recognize people from all identities and walks of life as "brothers and sisters," which is essential to respecting the dignity of another human being.[83] Seeing a person who is different from us

---

[81] Rahner identifies two levels of freedom: the categorical freedom that involves ability to choose between individual objects and transcendental freedom from which categorical freedom derives. See Mark O'Keefe, "Merton's 'True Self' and the Fundamental Option," *Merton Annual* 10 (1997); and Karl Rahner, *Foundations of Christian Faith* (New York: Crossroad, 1982), 90–115.

[82] US Conference of Catholic Bishops, *Open Wide Our Hearts*, 1.

[83] Ibid., 4.

as the Other conveys a mental and moral power of differentiation that makes violence possible.

One of the most distressing aspects of anti-Asian hate violence operating in our society today is that most of the victims are the elderly and women, and they are devalued by their Otherness and treated by their attackers as less than human. This was unmistakably demonstrated in one of the shocking attacks we examined—of a sixty-five-year-old Filipina in New York on March 29, 2021. The perpetrator treated Kari, a Filipina mother, like a virus by kicking her unprovoked and stomping on her head multiple times. Though he had never been a slave himself, the perpetrator, as a Black man, had likely adopted an anti-Asian mentality rooted in a long history of exclusionary nationalism, internalizing a White supremacist idea that dates back to the time of slavery by treating another human being as less-than-human. To add salt to the wound, the initial security footage showed that the entire incident took place in front of a building witnessed by a security guard who not only failed to render support, but actually closed the glass door of the building in reaction. Had he not wanted to get physically involved, he could have opened the door and yelled at the suspect who was less than a stone's throw away. Instead, he callously closed the door on Kari.[84]

Unfortunately, this scenario is repeated elsewhere. Attackers who are lacking moral human decency and bystanders who remain silent and say or do nothing—thereby, becoming complicit in the crime—occur on a regular basis in the United States today. In his encyclical *Fratelli Tutti* Pope Francis provides an example that eerily resembles the kind of violence that is occurring: "Someone is assaulted on our streets, and many hurry off as if they did not notice" (no. 65). He writes about what he

---

[84] Nicole Hong, Juliana Kim, Ali Watkins and Ashley Southall, "Brutal Attack on Filipino Woman Sparks Outrage: 'Everybody Is on Edge,'" *New York Times*, March 30, 2021, https://www.nytimes.com/2021/03/30/nyregion/asian-attack-nyc.html.

calls "symptoms of an unhealthy society" that "for all the progress we have made, we are still 'illiterate' when it comes to accompanying, caring for and supporting the most frail and vulnerable members of our developed societies. We have become accustomed to looking the other way, passing by, ignoring situations until they affect us directly" (no. 64). Perhaps these "symptoms of an unhealthy society" presage a gradual dissolution of a society, a disintegration of the traditional respect for the dignity of the human person codified in the Christian tradition. This is what happened when the markers of human decency or ethics have eroded to the extent that we are left with a country full of cowardly criminals who target the most vulnerable and gutless bystanders who remain silent in times of crises.

Out of these gruesome stories, however, come occasional stories of generosity and absolution. After a homeless White man, Jenkins, assaulted seventy-five-year-old Xiao Zhen Xie, her grandson set up a "Go Fund Me" page that raised more than a million dollars. To the surprise of many, Xie insisted on donating the whole fund to the Asian American community to combat anti-Asian racism.[85] Xie is a generous woman who was able to see beyond the immediate needs of herself and her family by striving to walk the extra mile to give something to her community. Her generous act reminds me of a story in Mark's gospel in which Jesus and his disciples were watching devotees as they entered the temple. It was customary for people to make an offering upon entering. Jesus and his disciples could hear the shekels of the wealthy as they cast their silver coins into the collection box. Then Jesus observed a poor widow dropping two small coins, and Jesus called his disciples over and told them: "I want you to observe that this poor widow

---

[85] Elisabetta Bianchini, "Elderly Asian Woman Who Fought Back Attacker Wants to Give Almost $900,000 in Donations to Asian American Community," *Yahoo News*, March 19, 2021.

contributed more than all the others" (Mk 12:44). Like the poor widow, Xie demonstrated the CST virtue of charity by giving not from her surplus but by disencumbering her new-found wealth for the sake of her people and community. She did not give lip service to peace and justice issues; instead, she gave herself to the task of unveiling the Kingdom of God in our midst.

But of all the victims mentioned above, Noel Quintana stood out as someone who was able to do something God-like that most would rebel at the thought of doing, because he was able to forgive the man who slashed his face with a box cutter. An interviewer asked Quintana, "Do you think you can forgive him for what he did?" and Quintana replied, "Oh yes, everybody deserves to have forgiveness." Quintana lives out one of the most unpalatable of Jesus's directive: to love our enemies as God loves even those who hate God.

Perhaps what enabled Quintana to forgive his attacker was that he did not allow himself to be identified with the hurts of being a victim, even though the scar across his face serves as a reminder of that horrific crime every time he looks in the mirror. Quintana does not allow what happened to him to become a defining point in his understanding of who he is. This is something that Elliot and other assailants are unable to do. They are unable to move on to a healthy anger about what happened to them. They wallow in their hurts and pains and allow them to define who they are. In the Christian tradition, people who are able to do what Quintana has done are considered holy. Quintana demonstrated the cornerstone of the CST principle of human dignity by living out the most unpalatable of Jesus's commandments in unequivocally forgiving the man who assaulted him.

The pastoral letter against racism distinguishes the notion of justice from that of injustice. In contrast to the original meaning of justice, "where we are in right relationship with God, with one

another, and with the rest of God's creation," St. Augustine's theological meaning of injustice is a "lust to dominate" the other.[86] If
lust to dominate is the original sin of humanity, as St. Augustine
puts it, then the antidote to injustice is empathy, which comes from
deep listening and identifying with the sufferings of others.[87] The
knowledge that comes from the understanding that Blacks and
Asian Americans are racially positioned in American society in
two different subordinations—Black/White binary and insider/
outsider spectrum, respectively—and detailed examples of what
took place in New York's Central Park between Amy Cooper
and Christian Cooper, and the series of incidents encountered by
Amara Walker at New Orleans International Airport serve as an
aid toward this deep listening process.

For many, however, it is hard to listen intently and to identify
with the sufferings of others during the spread of infectious disease.
The COVID-19 pandemic has produced a "lust to dominate"
through exclusionary nationalism (a sense that America is for Americans, and people of Asian descent are not part of it), triggering
attitudes and behaviors that include prejudice, racial intolerance,
and xenophobia. This has led to scapegoating, stigmatization, and
dehumanization of Asian Americans by equating them with the
virus itself. In *Fratelli Tutti*, Pope Francis reminds us that when challenged with violence in our society, we need to return to our sources,
to what is essential: "worship of God and love for our neighbor, lest
some of our teaching, taken out of context, end up feeding forms of
contempt, hatred, xenophobia or negation of others. The truth is
that violence has no basis in our fundamental religious convictions,
but only in their distortion" (no. 282).

---

[86] US Conference of Catholic Bishops, *Open Wide Our Hearts*, 6.
[87] Alison M. Benders, *Reading, Praying, Living the US Bishops' Open Wide
Our Hearts* (Collegeville, MN: Liturgical Press, 2018), 39.

3

Perpetual Foreigner

Chinese and other Asian ethnic groups were seen as aliens or foreigners in the United States long before the emergence of the model minority myth in 1966. And the psychocultural menace and racial and sexual fear associated with the yellow peril stereotype are predicated on the depiction of Asians and Asian Americans as outsiders who are alien Others and a threat to the Western way of life. The seemingly positive perceptions of Asian Americans as smart, hardworking, and successful, associated with the model minority myth, are balanced by the myth's shadow side of portraying Asian Americans as culturally and racially Other in the forever foreigner stereotype. The framers of the model minority myth gave it away with their right hand and took it back with their left. On one hand, it presents Asian Americans as hardworking and upwardly mobile and, on the other hand, categorizes them as unassimilable foreigners with little leadership quality, unable to be fully trusted in response to our supposed allegiance to our countries of origin.

The dismantling of these structures is essential for our acceptance as Americans. But to avoid repeating the history of the oppressed becoming the oppressor, Asian Americans need to seek their rightful place, recognized as full citizens of this country, by working in solidarity with other people of color.

As part of their 2021 Asian Americans and Pacific Islanders (AAPI) Heritage Month series, the New American Economy

Research Fund posted the latest data concerning the AAPI population in terms of the share of US-born versus foreign-born population of naturalized citizens, voter turnout at the 2020 presidential election, economic contributions of undocumented immigrants, and English language proficiency. The researchers are using this data to counter the depiction of AAPI as foreign outsiders and inescapably aliens. The article highlights that although immigration from Asia remains significant, "U.S.-born AAPI population is now growing faster than the AAPI immigrant population," with 45 percent of foreign-born AAPI residing in the United States for over twenty years; 4.7 percent of all eligible voters in the United States are AAPI; more than 84 percent of resettled refugees are naturalized citizens; and the share of limited English proficiency is higher for Hmong, Chinese, and Cambodian immigrants.[1] Although this data helps to dispel the myth that the AAPI population is mostly foreign-born, non-US citizens and, therefore, unable to vote, they do not combat "the AAPI perpetual foreigner stereotype," as stated in the title of the article.

To tackle the perpetual foreigner syndrome, we need to dismantle the various systems driven by the common ideology of White supremacy that uphold this engrained stereotype. One of those systems takes place at the level of interpersonal interaction where racial microaggressions have been encountered by AAPI.

System of Racial Microaggressions

Every person of Asian ancestry living in the United States, whether one is an immigrant or native to a country to which our forebears came many generations ago, has been asked, "Where are you from?"

---

[1] "Combating the AAPI Perpetual Foreigner Stereotype," *New American Economy Research Fund,* May 20, 2021, https://research.newamericaneconomy. org/report/aapi-perpetual-foreigner-stereotype/.

This may be a question of curiosity for those whose Americanness would never be called into question, but for Asian Americans
whose ethnicity is equated with foreignness, it implies that we are
not Americans and do not actually belong. The question is personal
enough that, if you are a native-born American of non-Asian
ethnicity, it should not be posed to a person of Asian heritage
whom you just met. As you get to know the person and are still
curious about where they are from, that would be an appropriate
time to ask—and it of course matters who is doing the asking.
When immigrants or foreign students from Asia ask this question
when they first meet Asian Americans, they are looking to connect
with their Asianness without dismissing the Americanness of their
Asian American identity. This is often not the case for those in the
dominant group because in cross-cultural encounters, they generally do not see the Americanness of Asian Americans or are not
interested in it—even though, according to the New American
Economy Research Fund, a third of the AAPI population are born
in this country.[2]

It is common for White Americans to question the nativity
of Asian Americans or compliment their English language proficiency: "Now, where are you really from?" or "Your English is
so good—you barely have any accent!" As Janette Ok, associate
professor of New Testament at Fuller Seminary, incisively stated
in her article "Always Ethnic, Never 'American': Reading 1 Peter
through the Lens of the 'Perpetual Foreigner' Stereotype," these
sorts of questions and compliments are subtle forms of racial
microaggressions, disguising "racism in seemingly benign and
well meaning behaviors and comments but convey the idea that
Asian Americans are less American and more foreign than their
white European counterparts." This association of Americanness
with Whiteness as a form of White supremacy is based on Cheryl

---

[2] Ibid.

Harris's important work on "whiteness as property" on how the construction of Whiteness as a type of racial identity has evolved into a kind of property. Ok demonstrates this in her chapter by examining a perplexing comment from a student's evaluation of her class when she was an adjunct professor many years ago. Despite positive appraisals of her teaching from her students, Ok was shocked by a student's disparaging remark in the comment section of her evaluation: "Instructor doesn't know how to speak English." As a native English speaker who was born and raised in the United States, Ok was stunned. She reflected that although she possesses the English fluency of a native speaker, from the student's perspective, she could not speak English the way a White person could. Ok writes, "This student felt entitled to assess my command of English because she understood English as her property, not mine. She judged my English proficiency through the lens of white supremacy."[3] In other words, even for Asian Americans who are born in the United States, holding a professional title and speaking English without a trace of a nonstandard accent, they can still be seen as a foreigner or non-American.

As Cynthia Choi, cofounder of Stop AAPI Hate puts it, "It's been a cold, sobering reminder that regardless of your immigration status, how many generations you've been here, we continue to have conditional status and to be 'othered.'"[4]

If a native speaker like Professor Ok receives a negative evaluation for her nonexistent English fluency problem, imagine what those who speak English with a more normative accent or a thick one must endure in their roles as teachers and public speakers. They

---

[3] Janette H. Ok, "Always Ethnic, Never 'American': Reading 1 Peter through the Lens of the 'Perpetual Foreigner' Stereotype," in *T & T Clark Handbook of Asian American Biblical Hermeneutics*, ed. Uriah Y. Kim and Seung Ai Yang (New York: T&T Clark, 2019), 419.

[4] Editorial Board, "Opinion: The Surge of Attacks Against Asian Americans Requires Attention and Swift Solutions," *Washington Post*, March 12, 2021.

are perceived as foreigners not only for their racialized bodies but also for their accented speech; this further marginalizes them as nonnational outsiders.

Accented Asian Americans in the teaching professions generally do not look forward to reading student evaluations for fear of finding vindictive comments about their "incomprehensible accent" or racist comments that question their legitimacy, role, and authority in the classroom. As teachers, they can recognize how these remarks often correlate with students' inaction or anxiety, for example, not keeping up with course readings; submitting hastily done, last-minute work; or other tensions that have nothing to do with their manner of speech or fluency in English. These are the kinds of pedagogical experiences, however, that are hard to explain to those who do not share their social locations and can become obstacles to their professional advancement. In addition, the tonal pattern of their speech can generate assumptions in some students, perhaps even among their colleagues, that they will never be as good as White professors. In this way, accents, language, and race often become the means to reify academic racial hierarchies. These hierarchies are most evident when people with European, Canadian, or Australian accents have been praised for having "beautiful" or "normal" accents by Americans in general, whereas people who speak English with an Asian accent have consistently elicited negative evaluations from American listeners.[5] This has to do with not only a lack of significant contact with Asian immigrants by Americans in a particular community but also with a long history of vicious and demeaning stereotypes in movies and popular culture

---

[5] Carina Bauman, "Social Evaluation of Asian Accented English," *University of Pennsylvania Working Papers in Linguistics* 19: no. 2: art. 3. In her study of mainstream US English, Asian–accented speakers, and Brazilian Portuguese–accented English, as well as her examination of other languages, Bauman supported her thesis that the perception of Asian accents is often outright negative.

that further reinforce the stereotype of Asian Americans as forever foreigners.

In *Forever Foreigners or Honorary Whites?*, Mia Tuan highlights the persistence of language-based prejudice when she recounts being teased with sing-song speech patterns that mimic supposed Asian languages that almost all Asian Americans experience growing up in this country. As in Professor Ok's case, this prejudice is not limited to those who speak English with an accent. Tuan provides an example in which former New York Senator Alfonse D'Amato, who was impatient with the progress of the high-profile O. J. Simpson murder trial in 1995, ridiculed Judge Lance Ito on Don Imus's nationally syndicated radio show by launching into a sing-song pidgin English mockery of Ito. Judge Ito, a *sansei* (third-generation Japanese American) was ridiculed as a foreigner with an Asian accent even though he was born and raised in Los Angeles and spoke English with no trace of a nonstandard accent.[6] This irresponsible mocking from a state senator only fed into the depiction of Asian Americans as those who occupy the marginal space of betwixt and between the two worlds of Asia and America without fully belonging to either.

Autobiography of Jung Young Lee

Jung Young Lee, Korean American theologian, exemplifies this sort of marginal experience in his autobiography. In "A Life In-Between: A Korean-American Journey," Lee recounts his experiences of marginality during the Korean War and his subsequent life as an immigrant in the United States.

The story begins with his visit to his native country of North Korea in the summer of 1991. Lee recalled how, in 1950, his father

---

[6] Mia Tuan, *Forever Foreigners or Honorary Whites? The Asian Ethnic Experience Today* (New Brunswick, NJ: Rutgers University Press, 2005), 1–3.

had taken him and his younger brother to the south with the intention of returning within a few weeks. The war, however, separated their family indefinitely. His mother decided to stay in Pyongyang because his seven-year-old brother Jung-yul broke his legs during the journey. The reunion with Jung-yul in 1991, more than forty years since he'd last seen him, was simultaneously joyful and heart-breaking as the pain of separation caused by the war created an "infinite emotional gap" between them that "could not be bridged by [their] short encounter."[7]

It was a disheartening realization that they would never be able to connect the way they would have if they had grown up together. The visit elicited attraction yet repulsion as his hometown had completely changed and the house in which he grew up had been replaced. His greatest disappointment was learning about the church built on the family property and money provided by his great grandmother, the matriarch of the family and first Christian in town, which no longer existed in an atheistic North Korea. Jung-yul told him that his mother, who had a formative influence on Lee's religious upbringing, blamed her husband for abandonment. This brought a great deal of sadness and guilt in Lee that he had not tried to physically connect with them sooner. His trip to his native land was necessary but also brought out the marginal feelings that he was visiting a place that had radically changed and where he no longer belonged, since people were suspicious of his American background and citizenship.

Lee came to the United States as a college student in 1955. The transition was particularly difficult as cultural differences and his inability to communicate in English led to misunderstandings

---

[7] Jung Young Kim, "A Life In-Between: A Korean-American Journey," in *Journeys at the Margin: Toward an Autobiographical Theology in American-Asian Perspective*, ed. Peter C. Phan and Jung Young Lee (Collegeville, MN: Liturgical Press, 1999), 25.

and incorrect interpretations of his homesickness from his sponsor and family. After his sponsors, husband and wife, picked him up from the airport, took him to their home, and gave him a tour of their house, he excused himself and went into his room for a much-needed rest. As soon as he got there, however, he began to sob as the loneliness of being in a strange country had reached an unbearable point. His sponsors took his despondency as ingratitude, and he was soon sent to another family.

Before graduating from college, Lee decided to enter seminary to become a minister. Lee's father, however, was opposed to his decision and disowned him. Bereft of his family, Lee's journey "was marked with loneliness, alienation, and suffering."[8] Then, after completing his theological education, he encountered racism within the church that was reflective of the wider racism in American society. Despite his qualifications, he was denied admission to full membership as an elder at the Ohio Conference of the Methodist Church because the Board of Ministerial Qualification did not think Lee would be appointable to a local church due to his race. This was the reality as no congregation in the conference wanted an Asian man as its pastor; instead, he was offered a janitorial job in a university church. Lee refused the offer, went back to school and found a part-time job as minister in an inner-city church. Later, he continued his education and eventually became a professor teaching at a small liberal arts college before moving to a state university and then, to a theological institution.

So, although he was a naturalized US citizen and lived most of his life in his adopted country, many Americans saw him on many levels as a foreigner. Wherever he went, people asked him, "When are you going home?" Living a life of in-betweenness, he was neither here nor there, betwixt and between North Korea and

---

[8] Ibid., 35.

the United States. He lived in what Victor Turner called a state of liminality. Taking inspiration from Turner's notion of liminality and reflecting on his experience of marginality, Lee developed a theology of marginality.

Theology of Marginality

As a seminal reflection on the quintessential Asian American experience, Lee's theology of marginality is helpful to understand Asian Americans grappling with their personal and cultural identities as the consequence of being portrayed as perpetual foreigners. The starting point for Lee's theology is autobiographical. In *Marginality: The Key to Multicultural Theology*, Lee writes, "Telling my story is not itself theology but a basis for theology, indeed the primary context for doing my theology. This is why one cannot do theology for another. If theology is contextual, it must certainly be at root autobiographical."[9]

Critics of the use of autobiography in academic studies point out the hermeneutical problem associated with self-reflection. In her defense of autobiographical theology against criticisms, Jung Ha Kim, senior lecturer at Georgia State University and a former student of Jung Young Lee, countered Hans-Georg Gadamer's argument that self-reflection and autobiography made history "private once more" and that "[t]he focus of subjectivity is a distorting mirror."[10] Kim masterfully responded, "To a person or community in need of recovering a sense of subjectivity due mainly to historical erasure, invisibility, and constant misrepresentation,

---

[9] Jung Young Lee, *Marginality: The Key to Multicultural Theology* (Minneapolis: Fortress Press, 1995), 7.

[10] Cited in Jung Ha Kim, "But Who Do You Say That I Am? (Matt 16:15): A Churched Korean American Women's Autobiographical Inquiry," in Phan and Lee, *Journeys at the Margin*. Hans-Georg Gadamer, *Truth and Method*, 2d rev. ed., trans. Joel Weinscheimer and Donald G. Marshall (New York: Crossroad, 1990), 276–7.

self-reflections and autobiographies are viable means of reclaiming wholeness, rather than producing privacy."[11] In other words, as a member of an Asian American community whose struggles and experiences have been misrepresented, erased, and made invisible in American history, Lee's autobiographical reflection, rather than producing privacy, resonates with every Asian American who has gone through similar experiences. In a sense, Lee helps Asian Americans recover their subjectivity by reflecting on the inevitable experience of marginalization with which every Asian American can identify. In so doing, he constructed a contextual theology of marginality comprising three stages: "In-between," "In-both," and "In-beyond."

In-Between Stage

The "In-between stage" describes the experience of those who are forced to live on the margins of the two worlds—in Lee's case, of Asia and America—yet never completely belonging to either. Asian Americans in this stage are estranged by Asians in Asia as being too Americanized, and in the United States, they are seen as being unassimilable, inscrutable, or possessing other stigmas of foreignness rendering them incapable of being American. In-betweenness means we occupy a space we would never be fully at home in. Lee relates this space of in-betweenness from his own experience of marginality:

> I am situated ambivalently between two worlds—America and Asia—and I absorb the repulsions and attractions or the rejection and acceptance of each. The marginal person has to live in these two worlds, which are not only different but often antagonistic to each other. From these two worlds, I chose membership in the dominant society, but it rejects me because of my root in the other world.

---

[11] Kim, "But Who Do You Say That I Am?, 111.

> Hence, I want to be accepted by the world of my ancestry,
> but it also rejects me. I am unwanted by both worlds, yet I
> live in them. That is why I am an absurd creature. . . . I am
> a part of two worlds without wholly belonging to either.[12]

He interprets this stage of in-betweenness in a negative sense. Those who live at the margins of both Asia and America, yet are never fully accepted in Asia or America, can suffer from a deep crisis of identity. An in-between state may arouse feelings of guilt for opposing or renouncing one's own culture or a sense of betrayal for adopting or surrendering to the dominant, mainstream culture. Furthermore, in-betweenness is rarely a matter of one's choice; rather, it is a space which Asian Americans are forced to occupy. In-betweenness is a coerced acceptance of one's existential condition of a marginal person as a consequence of those relegated to the margins of perpetual foreigners. To resist the narrative of the perpetual foreigner at the level of personal and cultural identity, one needs to cultivate identities that are derived from an "in-both" or "in-beyond" stage.

In-Both Stage

Asian Americans are not just "in-between" persons. We are also "in-both" persons in that both Asia and America are part and parcel of our makeup and identity. Asian Americans who embrace the "in-both" stage of their identity are comfortable and proud of a hybrid identity by not only recognizing the in-betweenness of their liminality but also acknowledging the in-bothness of their belonging. This means, Asian Americans are neither fully Asian nor fully American, yet both Asian and American. In-bothness is a positive and self-affirming aspect of Asian American identity.

---

[12] Lee, *Marginality*, 43–44.

Moreover, the ideas of in-betweenness and in-bothness are not unique to the Asian American experience. They are universal enough to be experienced by people of all races. Virgilio Elizondo, a Mexican American Roman Catholic priest and leading scholar of Hispanic theology, expressed an in-bothness in his autobiographical account:

> Between the school years at the seminary and the summers at the store, I gradually became more and more aware of the many things that I was not. I was not and would never be, even if I wanted to, a regular US-American. Yet neither would I be a *puro mexicano*. There were identities that I knew that I was and was not at the same time: US-American, Mexican, Spanish, Indian. Yet I was! My very being was a combination. I was a rich mixture but I was not mixed-up! In fact, I was more and more clear that my own inner identity was new and exciting. I started to enjoy the feeling of who I was: I was *not just* US-American and *not just* Mexican but fully both and exclusively neither.[13]

The in-bothness sense of belonging allows Elizondo to resist the discourse of perpetual foreignness by appropriating the process of interracial and intercultural mixing, or *mestizaje*, originally a denigrating label for the offspring of Amerindian and their Spanish conquerors, into a term of self-identity and cultural pride.

In-Beyond Stage

The "in-beyond" stage is an integration of the negative aspect of Asian Americans belonging in the world of neither Asia nor America ("in-between") and the positive aspect of belonging in the world of

---

[13] Virgilio Elizondo, *The Future Is Mestizo: Life Where Cultures Meet* (Bloomington, IN: Meyer-Stone Books, 1988), 26.

both Asia and America ("in-both"). Such integration enables Asian Americans to participate in both the world of their ancestors and the world of their residence without being bound by either. This constitutes a more mature state of marginality that Lee calls "new marginality," and persons who have reached this stage are referred to as "new marginal people." As Lee puts it, "To transcend or to live in-beyond does not mean to be free of the two different worlds in which persons exist, but to live in both of them without being bound by either of them."[14]

The questions "Where are you from?" or "Where are you really from?" are especially annoying for Asian Americans of second and later generations or, to use Mia Tuan's terminology, "Asian ethnics."[15] Since they are either born in this country or their family's roots in the United States go back many generations, they would like to be duly recognized as fully American. However, our racialized society frequently reminds them that they are marginal persons. They were either complimented for their English as if they were from another country, or asked, "Where are you really from?" In other words, it does not matter that Asian Americans are born here, or that they speak English without a trace of accent, or that they put their lives at risk by working in the health profession during this pandemic, they are still seen as perpetual foreigners.

To move to an "in-beyond" stage, we must recognize not only our in-betweenness but our in-bothness, and participate in both worlds of Asia and America without being bound by either. In my own autobiographical theological writing, I have reflected on the writings of Asian American cultural nationalists who emphasized the Americanness of their identity and downplayed their Asianness:

---

[14] Lee, *Marginality*, 63.
[15] Tuan, *Forever Foreigners*, 2.

The Americanness of our identity is something that we
choose and seek. We can be legally "American" by naturalization or by birth, but the structural and systemic
racism inherent in American society has blinded many in
the dominant group from recognizing us as authentically
American. The Asianness of our identity, however, is given
to us. It is not our choice to be Asians. We are born with
an Asian ethnicity. Often, the most important aspects of
our identity and our relationships are not those we choose,
but those with which we are born and have inherited. It is
within this context of what is natural born and not chosen
by us that we first learn to accept the "strangers" within
the Asian American subject—that is, our Asian roots and
differences in class, gender, and sexual preference.[16]

Asian ethnics cannot become what Lee called "a new marginal
person" by downplaying or ignoring their Asianness. To become a
new marginal person, they must come to terms not only with their
Americanness that they have sought to identify with but also with
the Asianness that they have not chosen.

Lee's Critique of Centrist Thinking

Julius-Kei Kato, associate professor of biblical and religious studies at
King's University College—Western University, astutely points out
that Lee's contextual theology, at its essence, consists of "a critique
of the situation in which a dominant group exercises hegemony over
all others" and of centralist thinking, which "is characterized by the
ideology of dominance" in which "the group at the center seeks to

---

[16] Joseph Cheah, "Life in the Fishbowl: An Asian American Autobio-
graphical Theological Reflection," in *Envisioning Religion, Race, and Asian
Americans*, ed. David K. Yoo and Khyati Y. Joshi (Honolulu: University of
Hawai'i Press, 2020), 202.

impose 'sameness' overall and suppress differences, and thus relegates to the margins groups or persons that do not conform to the central group's norms."[17] Lee opposes centralist forms of thinking and doing because it goes against the very design of God's creation. Lee considers centrism and centralist thinking an "ontic sin," which "is the root of oppression and marginalization in human society."[18] He considers plurality, especially in terms of racial and gender difference, constitutive of God's creation.

The perpetual foreigner stereotype is a product of centrism and centralist thinking in which the dominant group exercises hegemony over people of Asian descent by allowing this harmful stereotype to persist and permanently relegate Asian Americans to the margins of society. The damaging and lethal consequences of this ontic sin are at full display during times of crisis. During this pandemic, the depiction of Asian Americans as forever foreigners has made it possible for people to see Asians and Asian Americans as the Other, making it easier for bigots and racists to hold onto the illogical and absurd perception that all East Asians are carriers of COVID-19, and to justify acts of violence against Asians perceived to be Chinese.

As a product of centralist thinking, the perpetual foreigner stereotype has rendered the struggles of Asian Americans invisible to many non-Asian Americans. This is revealed in the ignorance of a significant percentage of White Americans to the plight of Asian Americans during the pandemic. The recent announcement by Leading Asian Americans to Unite for Change (LAAUNCH) of the findings of its recently developed STAATUS Index (Social Tracking of Asian Americans in the United States) "reveals 8 out of 10 Asian Americans say they are discriminated against in the

---

[17] Julius-Kei Kato, *How Immigrant Christians Living in Mixed Cultures Interpret Their Religion: Asian-American Diasporic Hybridity and its Implications for Hermeneutics* (Queenston, ON: Edwin Mellen Press, 2012), 161.

[18] Lee, *Marginality*, 107.

United States and 77% do not feel respected." In contrast, even with the increase in news coverage of recent anti-Asian attacks, "37% of white Americans, 46% of Republicans and 22% of Democrats say they aren't aware of the increase in assaults, hate crimes or other forms of racism against Asian Americans over the past year" and "24% of white Americans, 35% of Republicans and 12% of Democrats say they do not believe that anti-Asian American racism is a problem that should be addressed."[19] The last finding has as much, if not more, to do with the model minority myth as with the forever foreigner stereotype. In relation to the latter stereotype, "20% of survey respondents say Asian Americans are more loyal to their countries of origin than to the U.S." In other words, no matter how long we have been in the United States, the idea that Asians belongs in Asia is reflected in a seemingly benign but loaded question, "Where are you really from?"

System of Knowledge Dissemination

The uncritical presentation of Asian American history, when presented at all, in the nation's K–12 education is another way that deeply entrenched stereotypes are maintained. In her study of nine US history textbooks published between 1994 and 1996 for high school students in Hawaii, Violet Harada found textual references to Asian Americans ranged only from .56 percent to 2.1 percent in a state where the AAPI population constituted a whopping 61.8 percent in 1990.[20] In terms of the coverage of Chinese American history, all nine texts mentioned Chinese participation in the California Gold Rush, the construction of the transcontinental railroad,

---

[19] LAAUNCH, "Survey," *Associated Press News*, May 10, 2021.
[20] Campbell Gibson and Kay Jung, "Population Division: Historical Census Statistics on Population Totals by Race, 1790 to 1990, and by Hispanic Origin, 1970 to 1990, for the United States, Regions, Divisions, and States," *U.S. Census Bureau,* September 2002.

and the passage of the Chinese Exclusion Act of 1882. However, there was no in-depth treatment of these events. Chinese laborers were portrayed as passive rather than active agents in all the texts. They were described as "diligent and adaptive workers" who "risked their lives in performing some of the most dangerous tasks (e.g., being lowered in wicker baskets to set explosives)." None mentioned that they were active agents in standing up for their basic human rights to freedom from degrading treatment by organizing a strike to protest against inhumane working conditions in 1867.[21] In other words, Chinese American history becomes essentialized into a few easily identifiable events that obscure the active agents of Chinese laborers in resisting racist and unjust treatments.

While this study took place twenty-five years ago, the lower-tiered treatment of Asian American history in US history textbooks has not changed much. Amid the precipitous rise of anti-Asian violence during this pandemic, however, there has been a push by many states to include Asian American history in a model curriculum for public schools. In Connecticut, the language for HB6619 was amended to include Asian Pacific American studies as part of a model curriculum of AAPI studies in K–8, which was passed and signed by the Governor Ned Lamont in June 2021. For high school levels, there is currently a bipartisan bill (SB 678) to amend section 10-16b to include Asian Pacific American studies as part of the social studies curriculum. Some states, including California, are considering mandating ethnic studies programs; others are incorporating Asian American history into American history courses; still others are thinking about offering a survey course in which AAPI is one of the ethnic groups covered. On July 9, 2021, Governor J. B. Pritzker of Illinois signed into law the Teaching

    [21] Violet H. Harada, "The Treatment of Asian Americans in U.S. History Textbooks Published 1994–1996," Eric.ed.gov, Institution of Education Sciences, 16–17, files.eric.ed.gov/fulltext/ED448072.pdf.

Equitable Asian American Community History (TEAACH) Act. It requires all public elementary and high schools in Illinois, effective the 2022–2023 school year, to teach one unit on Asian American history, including the history of Asian Americans in Illinois and the Midwest, and the contributions of Asian Americans in advancing civil rights. In doing so, Illinois has become the first state to mandate Asian American history in public schools.[22] Hopefully, Catholic schools will follow the lead of a transformation that is beginning to take place in public schools across the nation.

Ideally, Asian American studies, African American studies, Native American studies, Chicano studies, and those of other minoritized groups should be included in American studies. The only reason we have separate histories of minoritized groups as a curriculum for general consumption is because they are systematically tokenized or excluded from the standard curriculum as if they are less than American. By amending the Illinois School Code to include Asian American history in public schools in Illinois, the TEAACH Act provides a better model curriculum for public schools than others, including the model initiated in Connecticut. Effective in fall 2022, Connecticut is the first state in the nation to offer African Americans, Black, Latino, and Puerto Rican Studies as elective courses. By making them an elective course of study, students who are not African Americans, Blacks, and Latinx, and would benefit from taking these courses, might not have the incentive to take them. Likewise, how many Latinx students after taking a course in Latino Studies or Puerto Rican Studies would opt to take a course in Black Studies and vice versa? The entire curriculum appears to be a form of appeasement from politicians to their most vocal constituents. While these courses will enable students to learn history that comes from their respective racial/ethnic

---

[22] "Pritzker Signs Law Making Illinois First State to Require Asian American History Be Taught in Schools," July 9, 2021, nbcchicago.com.

backgrounds, which is important, it does not necessarily prepare them to live in multicultural America.

To live and work in an increasingly multicultural and multiracial society, cultivation of racial literacy beyond one's own group is absolutely essential. It is no longer sufficient for our students to learn something about standard American history and a racialized history of their own racial/ethnic group. To receive an antiracism education, students must learn not only the standard history but also about the pivotal role the Black/White binary has played in American history and the ways in which White supremacy has operated in the histories of Latinx, Native Americans, Asian Americans, and other people of color. For example, understanding the fundamentals of African American history, including an appreciation of the alliances formed between Asian and African Americans during the Civil Rights Movement, will help Asian Americans better understand their own history. Similarly, understanding the history of hatred and violence against Chinese workers in the nineteenth century, including mob violence and lynching that endured even after the 1882 Chinese Exclusion Act, would help African Americans find historical solidarity in resisting White supremacy.[23] Understanding the different subordinations in which Black and non-Black minorities are racially positioned in the United States is crucial for cultivating racial literacy.

Connections between Black and Asian American Oppressions and Liberations

A much-anticipated livestream event on "Black and Asian Christians United against Racism," sponsored by Asian American Christian Collaborative, took place on April 5, 2021. Among the panelists was

---

[23] Joseph Cheah, "Racial Literacy, the Black-White Binary, and an Equitable Learning Environment," *Wabash Journal of Teaching and Learning* 2, no. 1 (2021): 119.

Reverend Otis Moss III, senior pastor of Trinity United Church of Christ in Chicago. In the spirit of Gary Okihiro's discussion about the parallels and conjoining struggles for freedom shared by Black and Asian Americans,[24] Reverend Moss spoke about the "unique thread" of racism that connects Black and Asian Americans.[25] I want to elaborate two of the examples he offered.

The first example has to do with the location of Asian Americans in a Black/White racial paradigm. Asian American historian Okihiro asks, "Is yellow black or white?" For Okihiro, Asian Americans were "near black" in the past and "near-white" in the present, but "yellow is emphatically neither white nor black."[26] Frank Wu, former distinguished law professor and the current president of Queens College, said Asian Americans have been treated for most of the country's history as primarily "constructive blacks."[27] Indeed, the California Supreme Court in 1854 declared that Asian Americans were "blacks" or at least "constructive blacks" in the case concerning *People v. Hall*. George Hall, a White man, was convicted and sentenced to death after three Chinese witnesses testified that Hall murdered Ling Sing, a Chinese miner in Nevada County. It should be noted that William Stewart, the prosecutor, took pains to ensure that Chinese miners could testify by securing additional funds and recruiting a Presbyterian missionary, Reverend Speer, to serve as an interpreter. However, in 1854, Chief Justice Hugh Murray overturned the conviction, holding that Chinese eyewitness testimony against a White man was inadmissible

---

[24] Gary Y. Okihiro, *Margins and Mainstreams: Asians in American History and Culture* (Seattle: University of Washington Press, 1994), 58.

[25] Emily McFarlan Miller, "Black and Asian Christian Church Leaders Discuss Role of Church in Fighting Racism," *Religion News Service*, April 6, 2021.

[26] Okihiro, *Margins and Mainstreams*, 34.

[27] Angelo N. Ancheta, *Race, Rights, and the Asian American Experience*, 2d edition (New Brunswick, NJ: Rutgers University Press, 2006), 5.

because the Chinese were "'a race of people whom nature has marked as inferior, and who are incapable of progress or intellectual development beyond a certain point' and as such had no right 'to swear away the life of a citizen' or participate 'with us in administering the affairs of our Government.'"[28] This decision rendered Chinese "Black" for the purpose of political disenfranchisement.

Reverend Moss made the connection that *People v. Hall* provided a blueprint for the 1857 legal case involving *Dred Scott v. John F.A. Sandford* in which the Supreme Court ruled that "a slave (Dred Scott) who had resided in a free state and territory (where slavery was prohibited) was not thereby entitled to his freedom; that African Americans were not and could never be citizens of the United States."[29] While making this connection, it is important to recognize that the experience of being Black in the United States is not the same as the experience of being Asian in the same country. While the California Supreme Court categorized the Chinese on the same level as Black or, as Wu puts it, constructive or implied Black, they were not exactly the same as Blacks who were seen as property. More importantly, while the Chinese experienced horrific violence in American history, they were not enslaved for over 250 years, as were African Americans. Although Black and Asian Americans experienced different forms of oppression, Reverend Moss reminded us that they are linked together, as *People v. Hall*'s case served as a model for the US Supreme Court's Dred Scott decision.

Another example Reverend Moss offered is the connection between the Chinese Massacre of 1871 and the subsequent lynching of Blacks across the country.[30] In 1871, the worst mass

---

28   Immigration History, "People v. Hall (1854)," ImmigrationHistory.org.

29   "Dred Scott Decision," https://www.Britannica.com/event/Dred-Scott-decision.

30   Miller, "Black and Asian Christian Church Leaders Discuss Role of Church in Fighting Racism."

lynching in US history took place in Los Angeles when rival brokers of two Chinese companies—Nin Yung Company and Hong Chow Company—had a feud over the kidnapping of a runaway prostitute, Ya Hit. The shootout between the leaders of these two competing groups and the ensuing violence, followed by the beginning of a lynching spree, inadvertently resulted in the death of a White civilian and the wounding of a police officer. Subsequently, a mob of rioters quickly descended upon the scene, and when the violence was over, seventeen Chinese men and boys were lynched and two others were knifed to death, even though only one participated in the shootout.[31]

In the West, from the mid-nineteenth to the early twentieth century, lynching had served as a form of vigilante justice. Of the estimated 302 lynchings that occurred in California from 1849 to 1902, about 200 victims of lynching were of Asian descent.[32] The Chinese Massacre, according to Reverend Moss, provided a blueprint for continued lynchings of Black Americans in the South and across the country. It should be noted that in 1872, a year after the Chinese Massacre, the California state legislature granted Chinese residents the right to testify against Whites in court, nearly a decade after California's African Americans had won that right.[33] In this case, the right of African Americans to testify against Whites became a model for the same right granted to the Chinese. Hence, not only is the oppression of Black and Asian Americans linked together but also their liberation.

Reverend Moss also pointed to the example of the Azusa Street Revival in 1906 as proof that "the Spirit functions in a way that

---

[31] Kelly Wallace, "Forgotten Los Angeles History: The Chinese Massacre of 1871," *Los Angeles Public Library*, May 19, 2017.

[32] Jean Pfaelzer, *Driven Out: The Forgotten War against Chinese Americans* (New York: Random House, 2007), 47–49, 54.

[33] Josh Paddison, *American Heathens: Religion, Race, and Reconstruction in California* (Berkeley: University of California Press, 2012), 42.

white supremacy could not control."[34] The Azusa Street Revival in 1906 is considered by many as the beginning of Pentecostalism worldwide. Since the late twentieth century, Pentecostalism has been the fastest growing Christian denomination, especially in the Global South.[35] Perhaps this gives credence to Reverend Moss's assertion that the 1906 Azusa Street Revival led by Black, Asian, and Latino Christians was successful beyond imagination as Pentecostalism has been spreading like wildfire in the Global South because the Spirit blows where it wills, and White supremacy is powerless to control it. I now extend Reverend Moss's theme that the oppression of Black and Asian Americans are connected by providing additional examples and an example of how our liberation is linked together.

Sometimes discrimination against African Americans provides a blueprint for that of Asian Americans, as in the 1927 US Supreme Court case, *Gong Lum v. Rice*. In 1924, Gong Lum enrolled his native-born, nine-year-old daughter, Martha Lum, in an all-White Rosedale Consolidated School in Bolivar County, Mississippi. At noon recess, however, the school superintendent, acting on an order issued by the board of trustees, called Martha into her office to tell her that she would not be allowed to return to the school because she was not a member of the White or Caucasian race. Martha's father, Gong Lum, initiated litigation. A state court directed school officials to readmit Martha because it held that she should not have been categorized as "colored." The Supreme Court of Mississippi then reversed that decision, citing that Martha was of "the Mongolian or yellow race" and therefore could not attend a White school. When the case reached the US Supreme Court

---

[34] Miller, "Black and Asian Christian Leaders Discuss Role of Church in Fighting Racism."

[35] Edmund Kee-Fook Chia, *World Christianity Encounters World Religions: A Summa of Interfaith Dialogue* (Collegeville, MN: Liturgical Press, 2018), 17–18.

in 1927, Chief Justice William Howard Taft cited a long list of cases including *Cumming v. Richmond County Board of Education* (1899), which upheld separate high schools for Black and White students, and *Plessy v. Ferguson* (1896), which upheld the "separate but equal" doctrine in public education.[36] These two cases became the bases for the Supreme Court ruling that Chinese were non-White and thus were not allowed to attend schools reserved for Whites. *Both Cumming v. Richmond County Board of Education* (1899) and *Gong Lum v. Rice* (1927) would later be overturned by another landmark US Supreme Court decision in *Brown v. Board of Education* (1954).

Several decades earlier, a case concerning Mamie Tape, an eight-year-old Chinese American girl, provided a blueprint for challenging racial segregation in public schools. It was in September 1884 that Joseph and Mary McGladery Tape, a one and-a-half generation middle-class Chinese American couple, tried to enroll their eldest daughter, Mamie, at the all-White Spring Valley Primary School. Principal Jeannie Hurley and the San Francisco school board refused to admit her, citing state education codes that allowed schools to exclude students characterized as having "filthy or vicious habits, or children with contagious disease." Faced with this racist policy, at a time when Chinese workers became a convenient scapegoat for the widespread economic depression in the United States, Joseph and Mary Tape filed a lawsuit against both Hurley and the San Francisco board of education. A San Francisco superior court judge agreed with the Tapes' attorney, William Gibson, son of the Reverend Otis Gibson, that the equal protection clause of the Fourteenth Amendment that granted Mamie equal access to free education in public school had been violated. While the Tapes won the lawsuit, the superior court judge did

---

[36] Mark A. Gooden, "Gong Lum v. Rice," *Britannica*, https://britannica.com/event/Gong-Lum-v-Rice.

not allow Mamie to attend an all-White school and established
a separate Chinese primary school for Mamie and other Chinese
students to attend.[37]

When the new school year began in 1885 and the new
Chinese-only school was not quite ready to open, the Tapes again
sought to enroll Mamie at Spring Valley School. Hurley refused
again, citing that the classroom was already too crowded and
that Mamie did not have her proper vaccination certifications.
In response, Mary Tape wrote an enraged letter to the *Alta California* newspaper. "Will you please tell me! Is it a disgrace to be
born a Chinese? Didn't God make us all!!!" Throughout the litigation, the Tapes presented themselves as Christians seeking to live
the American dream. They used their Christianity to challenge
racial segregation while underscoring the superiority of Christian
marriage, the English language, and American culture.[38] It was only
after *Tape v. Hurley* that an increasing number of Chinese children
began attending White schools in San Francisco, even though
the California law authorizing separate Chinese public schools
remained on the books.[39]

Now, fast forward again to *Brown v. Board of Education*.
What Joseph and Mary Tape did for their daughter Mamie was
repeated nearly seventy years later when an African American
plaintiff named Oliver Brown, on behalf of his daughter Linda,
filed a class action suit against the Board of Education of Topeka,
Kansas, in 1951. In his lawsuit, Brown put forth that Black schools
and White schools were not equal, and that segregation violated
the equal protection clause of the Fourteenth Amendment, which

---

[37] Erika Lee, *The Making of Asian America* (New York: Simon and
Schuster, 2015), 83.

[38] Paddison, *American Heathens*, 180.

[39] Sarah Pruitt, "The 8-year-old Chinese American Girl Who Helped
Desegregate Schools—in 1885," History.com, March 16, 2021.

states that no state can "deny to any person within its jurisdiction the equal protection of the laws."[40] The case eventually went to the US Supreme Court, which cited both the 1896 landmark decision of *Plessy v. Ferguson* and the 1927 case of *Gong Lum v. Rice* as precedents, and ruled unanimously that racial segregation in public schools violated the Fourteenth Amendment.

While oppression of Black and Asian Americans is not the same, their "threads of racism" are linked together by pitting one group against the other. As Richard Delgado and Jean Stefancic point out in *Critical Race Theory,* in American history, when one group is gaining ground, another is often losing it.[41] The Naturalization Act of 1870 extended US citizenship to "aliens of African nativity and to persons of African descent" while the Senate expressly rejected an amendment to permit Chinese immigrants to be naturalized US citizens. This was confirmed in the 1878 landmark court decision that deemed the Chinese plaintiff Ah Yup, a native of China, a person of Mongolian descent, was not entitled to become a naturalized citizen of the United States.[42] Furthermore, nowhere is White supremacy more evident than in the use of the 1870 Naturalization Act to prevent immigration of Chinese women who have marital partners in the United States. What does the extension of naturalization to Blacks have to do with the banning of Chinese women from uniting with their spouses? Nothing, except White supremacy operates by ensuring not all minoritized groups gain ground at the same time. Moreover, in 1875, Congress passed the Page Act to prevent all Chinese women,

---

[40] "Brown v. Board of Education," History.com, May 13, 2021.

[41] Richard Delgado and Jean Stefancic, *Critical Race Theory: An Introduction* (New York: New York University Press, 2012), 79.

[42] Ian F. Haney Lopez, *White by Law: The Legal Construction of Race* (New York: New York University Press, 1996), 5–6. In Ah Yup's case, the courts used two rationales to justify their decisions: common knowledge and scientific evidence.

under the pretext of "Mongolian" prostitutes, from entering the
United States and, in 1882, Congress terminated Chinese laborer
immigration altogether.

Normalization of Racial and Social Injustice

Patricia Hill Collins, a noted sociologist and Black feminist, defines
"controlling images" as "images [that] are designed to make racism,
sexism, poverty, and other forms of social injustice appear to be
natural, normal, and inevitable parts of everyday life."[43] Accord-
ingly, in her book, *Black Feminist Thought*, Collins describes the
controlling image of mammy, an enduring southern racial caricature
of African American women, as "the faithful, obedient domestic
servant" who nurtured and cared for the children of her White
"family" better than her own. She adds, "A mammy symbolizes the
dominant group's perceptions of the ideal Black female relationship
to elite White male power." No matter how well loved, and although
she "may wield considerable authority in her White 'family,' mammy
knows her 'place' as obedient servant." Such an expectation still
exists today when Black professional women are expected to exhibit
a mammy character by putting on a veil of geniality and display
deferential behavior because "[m]ammy is the public face that
Whites expect Black women to assume for them."[44] A well-known
advertising character that reinforces this stereotype is the Aunt
Jemima brand of pancake and syrup that its Quaker Oats–owned
company has recently replaced.

Collins's discussion of the mammy's controlling image reminds
me of another controlling image of a Filipina domestic servant
in Alex Tizon's article "My Family's Slave." The author tells a

---

[43] Patricia Hill Collins, *Black Sexual Politics: African Americans, Gender,
and the New Racism* (New York: Routledge, 2004), 69.

[44] Patricia Hill Collins, *Black Feminist Thought: Knowledge, Consciousness,
and the Politics of Empowerment* (New York: Routledge, 1999), 72–73.

story of his family's nanny and domestic servant, Eudocia Tomas Pulido, who was a distant relative of Tizon, born into a much poorer family. Her poverty ultimately led her to some difficult life choices. Rather than attending school, Eudocia worked her entire life and was expected to marry a pig farmer more than twice her age when she reached the age of eighteen. In order to escape this arrangement, she opted to serve the Tizon family as a caretaker for generations of their children in exchange for food and shelter. Years later, when Tizon's father was offered a job in foreign affairs as a commercial analyst, Eudocia was asked to accompany the Tizons to America with the promise of better working conditions and an allowance to send back home to her parents and other relatives in the village. Eudocia left her family behind, contingent upon promises that Tizon's parents would never fulfill.

The transition from the Philippines to the United States was especially traumatic for Eudocia. She worked long hours, ate leftovers by herself in the kitchen, had no friends or hobbies apart from the family, no private room she could call her own, frequently slept among piles of laundry, and was often emotionally abused by Tizon's mother. Before leaving diplomatic work, Tizon's father secured permanent residency status for his family but kept Eudocia tied to them as their personal domestic worker without security in her own residency. This left her in a situation in which she could easily be exploited and forced to be hidden from the outside world for fear of deportation or abandonment by her only connections in the United States.

This also protected the Tizons who were compelled not to follow fair labor practices because her services were rendered behind closed doors, making her a modern-day slave.[45] Despite being a key part of the Tizon family, called *"Lola,"* or "Grandma" in Tagalog by her children, her isolation that gradually increased

---

[45] Alex Tizon, "My Family's Slave," *The Atlantic*, July 2017.

throughout her life and the way she was treated by the Tizons created what Rachel Bundang called "unintelligible cruelty." Because of her illiteracy, Eudocia's story was told not by her but from the perspective of a male member of the Tizon family who had not experienced her situation firsthand. Alex Tizon gave his account by coming to terms with what had happened, attempting to reconcile with his past. He confronted his and his family's complicity with unethical situations in relation to Lola by airing his family's dirty laundry, which would make both his family and Filipinos as a whole look "morally backward" in the process. On the other hand, he shed light about this injustice and let the world know in a way that "challenges Filipinos and others to take a moral stock of how we actually treat the least among us and how we—if we claim to be people of faith and conscience—must absolutely take respect for human dignity seriously."[46]

Acceptance of cheap labor that is often tantamount to slavery, and allowing people in power to bend the rules, is what makes stories like Eudocia's possible. It was not just Tizon's family who failed her. Both the systems in the Philippines and in the United States failed her. Since we are part of the system, we are all complicit in the existence of these practices. We are complicit when we do not hold accountable individuals and corporations who are known to exploit cheap labor, or when we vote for politicians and policies that support or refuse to improve labor practices. Like the exploitation of mammys in Collins's example, domestic workers are vulnerable to abuse and exploitation when labor laws and other forms of protection are found wanting. Both cases are examples of ontic sin. They are part of a system that perpetuates the dehumanization of people living at the margins of society.

---

[46] Rachel Bundang, "Unintelligible Cruelty," in *Critical Theology: Engaging Church Culture Society*, ed. Rosemary P. Carbine, 2, no. 1 (Fall 2019): 19–20.

Conclusion and Theological Reflection

Concerning migrants, strangers, and foreigners, the book of Deuteronomy speaks directly to American people: "you too must befriend the alien, for you were once aliens yourselves" (Dt 10:19). With the exception of Native Americans, who have been in North America for millennia, the rest of us are settlers and forced or voluntary migrants. The author of Deuteronomy challenges us to care for the migrants in our midst, for our forebears were all once migrants themselves. Elsewhere in the Bible, in the book of Hebrews, we hear, "Do not neglect hospitality, for through it some have unknowingly entertained angels" (Heb 13:2). It is, therefore, no surprise that Catholic Church documents, from Pope Leo XIII's 1891 *Rerum Novarum* to Pope Francis's 2020 *Fratelli Tutti* appeal to the world to respond to migrants and foreigners with compassion.

As a nation of immigrants, our historical record in treating immigrants and foreigners in our midst is much to be desired. This is patently seen in the legal construction of Chinese as aliens and "constructive Blacks" in the nineteenth and early twentieth centuries. When the California Supreme Court overturned the murder of the Chinese miner, Ling Sing, by George Hall in 1854, Chief Justice Murray not only racialized Chinese as "constructive Blacks" by rendering them as less than human, declaring them to be "a race of people whom nature has marked as inferior,"[47] but also legalized violence against Chinese who could no longer testify against Whites. The ruling created an open season of violence against the Chinese who were without legal recourse to protect themselves. The message was that if Hall got away with murder, so could any White man since legal testimony by the Chinese against Whites was no longer admissible in court. The ruling encouraged or made

---

[47] "People v. Hall (1854)," Immigrationhistory.org, University of Texas at Austin Department of History.

it easier to commit violence against the Chinese, exemplified in the 1871 "Chinese Massacre" and mob violence during the economic depression of the 1870s.

Many actors and groups were complicit in the system that perpetuated the dehumanization of the Chinese: the legal establishment that rendered them voiceless and without legal protection, the government-sponsored discrimination that ignored their basic rights to be treated as humans, the callousness of many Irish who used their voting power to ban Chinese immigration to the United States altogether, and the nonresponse of bystanders in the hierarchy of the Catholic Church in the nineteenth century.

The treatment of Chinese and, later, other Asians as forever foreigners was actively enforced not only in the verdict of *People v. Hall* but in many federal laws, including antimiscegenation laws between Whites and Asians in fifteen states across the country. Because there were very few women of Chinese descent in the United States, many Chinese men who wanted to start a family went back to China to find a wife. Some would attempt to smuggle women from China in arranged marriages to the United States to meet their immigrant husbands to whom they would marry by "proxy." But since it was extremely difficult to sponsor a Chinese woman to the United States at that time, many men who decided to settle in their adopted land often married outside their race. Depending on where they settled, Chinese migrants tied knots with African American, Native American, Mexican, and Native Hawaiian women. In Mississippi, where prohibitions to White intermarriage applied not only to Blacks but also "Mongolians to the third generation," Chinese men frequently married African American women.[48] In New York City, during the 1860s and

---

[48] Leslie Bow, *Asian Americans and Racial Anomaly in the Segregated South* (New York: New York University Press, 2010), 48–49.

1870s, the most common interracial marriages were between Chinese immigrant men and poor Irish immigrant women.[49]

The specter of miscegenation was so powerful that it was nearly impossible for Chinese men to marry White women and was particularly difficult for White women to marry Chinese men not simply because it was taboo, and could arouse outrage and humiliation, but also the nation itself legally forbade interracial marriages. In terms of absolute numbers, interracial marriages between Asian men and White women were not many, but enough for the states to enact antimiscegenation laws and for the Congress to pass the Married Women's Citizenship Act, more commonly known as the Expatriation Act in 1907, decreeing that any American woman (read: White women) who married a foreign national would lose her citizenship. An American woman married to a Chinese would lose not only her citizenship but would also assume her husband's nationality, and the terms of the Chinese Exclusion Act would apply to her as well.[50] This was a warning to White women that they would be removed from the White racial body and turned into aliens by means of a legal sleight of hand. Such laws and acts patently reveal that race and gender were dominant factors in the formation of state policies with respect to the treatment of Chinese and other AAPI in the United States.

Letticie Pruett exercised her basic human right to find a soulmate when she violated the antimiscegenation law and married Fong See, a successful businessman, in 1897. To be expected, Pruett was disowned by her family for marrying a Chinese.

Fong See's father came to the United States in 1867. He opened an herbal store "where he prescribed herbal remedies to immigrant laborers who were treated little better than slaves."

---

[49] Lee, *The Making of Asian America*, 79, 83.

[50] Eric Fish, Interview with Emma J. Teng, "How Mixed Chinese-Western Couples Were Treated a Century Ago," *Asia Society*, January 10, 2017.

See came to America as a youngster and, later, became one of the richest Chinese individuals in the country.[51] The great grand-daughter of Fong and Letticie, Lisa See, has spent years of research chronicling the one-hundred-year odyssey of her Chinese American family in *On Gold Mountain*. In spite of the antimiscegenation law, the 1907 Expatriation Act and the 1922 Cable Act, both of which were enacted to maintain the boundary between Whites and Asians, the Chinese American history, as Lisa See puts it, is about her family representing "a history that encompasses racism, romance, secret marriages, entrepreneurial genius, and much more, as two distinctly different cultures meet in a new world."[52]

While *Encountering Christ in Harmony* and *Open Wide Our Hearts* do not directly address the complexity of the convergence of foreignness and race with respect to the experience of AAPI, Pope Francis in *Fratelli Tutti* uses the parable of the Good Samaritan to expand our hearts to embrace the foreigner in our midst: "Every brother or sister in need, when abandoned or ignored by the society in which I live, becomes an existential foreigner, even though born in the same country. They may be citizens with full rights, yet they are treated like foreigners in their own country" (no. 97). This speaks directly to the kind of racism experienced by AAPI for they have been treated as perpetual "foreigners in their own country." To be treated as forever foreigners in their own country leads to being treated as objects to be ignored, bullied, harassed verbally and physically, because they are seen as outsiders and second-class citizens.

This is another instance of blaming the victim. Not only were the Chinese prevented from entering the United States, but the US Supreme Court held that those who remained in the country could

---

[51] Lisa See, *On Gold Mountain: The One-Hundred-Year Odyssey of My Chinese-American Family* (New York: Vintage Books, 1995), 56–58.

[52] Ibid.

not become naturalized US citizens. So even if the Chinese had wanted to, they could not become full members of the national body. The perception of Chinese and other Asian Americans as "aliens ineligible for citizenship" was used as a proxy for their exclusion from the national body.

Such an exclusion would not be bound by those ineligible for citizenship. The incarceration of Japanese Americans during World War II taught us the tragic lesson that Japanese Americans who were born in the United States were denied their place in the national body and were sent to concentration camps. According to Lee's marginal theology, Japanese Americans found themselves in a state of in-betweenness in which they were neither part of the US national community nor did they have an imagined homeland to which to return. This exemplifies their precarious position during this period of American history.

This sort of liminal state in which Asian Americans found themselves is what Jung Young Lee called the in-between state in his marginal theology. At the level of personality development, Lee's "in-between," "in-both," and "in-beyond" stages complement "traditionalist," "marginal man," and "Asian-American" typological characters posited by Stanley Sue and Derald Wing Sue in their 1973 chapter "Chinese-American Personality and Mental Health." A "traditionalist" is a person of Asian heritage who has strongly internalized the Asian values of allegiance to the family into which they are born, obedience to their parents, and success in educational achievement and occupational status. A "marginal man" struggles with a form of "racial self-hatred" as he rejects Asian culture and values in favor of the values and behavior of the dominant group. It should be noted that the "marginal man" character in Sue and Sue is different from a "new marginal person" in Lee's typology. The third typological character, "Asian-American," integrates elements from both Asian and American cultures in ways that are functional to the person's self-esteem and identity.[53] Both "traditionalist" and "marginal man" characters can be found in a person undergoing in-between and in-both stages, whereas an authentic "Asian-American" character can only be found in a person who has achieved the "new marginality" of the "in-beyond" stage.

At a structural level, the system of normalization of racial and social injustice is accomplished through what Collins called "controlling images." They are designed to make uncritical presentation of the AAPI histories in the system of knowledge dissemination and stereotypical representations of AAPI in the system of racial microaggressions to appear normal and an unavoidable part of everyday life. AAPI histories and experiences in high school textbooks or in church documents often received lower-tier treatment, with the obligatory one to two paragraphs that portray AAPI as passive agents in their histories. This passivity is reinforced in media representations of Asian men as effeminate, desexualized, and socially inept, whereas Asian women are depicted either as docile, passive, and submissive ("lotus blossom" stereotype) or aggressive, manipulative, and seductive ("dragon lady" stereotype). All of these representations are further reinforced in the system of racial microaggressions that lead to the perpetuation of AAPI as the forever foreigner.

One way to resist these representations is to recognize and educate the existence of the "threads of racism" that connect all people of color together and how often they are pitted against each other to protect White privilege and supremacy. Reverend Moss reminds us that Black and Asian Americans have the "unique thread" of racism that connects them together, and would assist

---

[53] Stanley Sue and Derald Wing Sue, "Chinese-American Personality and Mental Health," in *Asian-Americans: Psychological Perspectives*, ed. Stanley Sue and Nathaniel N. Wagner (Palo Alto, CA: Science and Behavior Books, Inc., 1973), 113–17.

them in finding historical moments of solidarity in resisting White supremacy. As Okihiro puts it, African and Asian Americans are kindred people: "We share a history of colonization, oppression and exploitation, and parallel and mutual struggles for freedom. We are a kindred people, forged in the fire of white supremacy and tempered in the water of resistance."[54] It is therefore imperative to teach the shared histories of oppression and liberation of all people of color.

Among Black and Asian Americans, it is important to recognize how the 1871 Chinese Massacre served as a template for thousands of lynchings in the South, how the 1882 Chinese Exclusion Act served as a blueprint for the separate but equal decision of the 1896 *Plessy v. Ferguson* decision, and how the lawsuit filed by an Asian American couple, Joseph and Mary Tape, to admit their daughter into an all-White primary school in 1884 was repeated in 1951 when an African American parent, Oliver Brown, filed a class action suit that finally led the Court to determine that Black and White schools were not equal. Moreover, when a racialized group fights for their rights and self-determination, they help lift other minoritized groups as well. As we saw in chapter 2, the civil rights that AAPI enjoy today were made possible by the African Americans fighting for their own rights.

In the spirit of African Americans who fought for birthright citizenship in antebellum America, Wong Kim Ark's contribution to the civil rights of all Americans is one of the most neglected cases in American history. Born in San Francisco, California, in 1873 to Chinese immigrant parents who were ineligible to become US citizens, Wong made several trips to China, first with his parents and later, as a young adult. In 1894, he traveled to China for a temporary visit. On his return trip in 1895, immigration officers barred his reentry on the grounds that Chinese immigrants

---

[54] Okihiro, *Margins and Mainstreams*, 60–61.

could not receive citizenship by "mere accident of birth" and that children of parents ineligible for citizenship could not receive citizenship by birthright. He was imprisoned on a ship in San Francisco Bay for four months, and then spent another three years out on bail suing for his citizenship as his case made its way up to the US Supreme Court. Realizing that the future of birthright citizenship was at stake for all children of noncitizens, Wong won his case of birthright citizenship by connecting his claim to citizenship not just to his own or to Chinese children but to children of White immigrants. In effect, he was forced to fight for the rights of White immigrants in order to have his own rights and those of Chinese children recognized by proxy.[55]

Wong's landmark victory won the rights for every child born in the United States regardless of race or nationality, even those born to parents ineligible for naturalization, to be recognized as citizens under the Fourteenth Amendment.[56] Wong's legal victory has helped millions of Americans since his time. Teaching the shared histories of oppression and liberation across different racial and ethnic groups is an essential element of cultivating an antiracist society.

---

[55] Amanda Frost, "Birthright Citizens and Paper Sons: The Complicated Case of an American-born Child of Chinese Immigrants," *American Scholar*, January 18, 2021.

[56] Lee, *The Making of Asian America*, 84–85.

Conclusion

This book supplements the invisibility of the history and experiences of Asian Americans and Pacific Islanders (AAPI) in *Open Wide Our Hearts*[1] and challenges a wholly inadequate representation of Asian American history in *Encountering Christ in Harmony*.[2] It does so by attending to Asian American concerns so intricately coded into the experience that one would have difficulty cracking the cipher without examining the three toxic stereotypes—namely, yellow peril, the model minority, and the perpetual foreigner—that have detrimentally impacted the lives of AAPI in general and Asian Americans in particular. These harmful stereotypes have been examined in detail in chapters 1, 2, and 3. In this concluding chapter, we explore the scriptural portrayal of Jesus's experience of these three destructive stereotypes, the theological emphasis on the good news for the poor, and the value of the Catholic Social Teaching (CST) principles reflected in the practices of AAPI community-based organizations.

---

[1] US Conference of Catholic Bishops, *Open Wide Our Hearts: The Enduring Call to Love—A Pastoral Letter Against Racism* (Washington, DC: USCCB, 2018).

[2] US Conference of Catholic Bishops, *Encountering Christ in Harmony: A Pastoral Response to Our Asian and Pacific Island Brothers and Sisters* (Washington, DC: USCCB, 2018).

What We Know about Jesus

We find both the Christ of faith and the Jesus of history in the Gospels, which means the Gospels were written not primarily to give a biographical or historical account of Jesus but to lead people of faith to Jesus as Lord and Savior. It also means that Jesus, God's incarnate, became a human being like us in all things except sin (Heb 4:15) and was no stranger to similar kinds of toxic stereotypes experienced by Asian Americans of the past and the AAPI of today.

What little we know about the birth of Jesus and his formative years comes primarily from the Gospels of Luke and Matthew. While they offer two different accounts of those early years, they both agree that Jesus was born in Bethlehem and that he grew up in Nazareth in the territory of Galilee, a region known for being unsophisticated and Gentile. In the Gospel of Matthew, Joseph, Mary, and Jesus became refugees, fleeing to Egypt to escape Herod's murderous plot to rid himself of competition to the throne by killing all infants in and around Bethlehem because three visitors from the East were seeking the newborn king of the Jews (Mt 2:1–18). After Herod's death, Joseph was afraid to return to Judea because Herod's son, Archelaus, was the new king; instead, they went and dwelt in a town called Nazareth in the region of Galilee (Mt 2:19–23). Their return to Nazareth hardly foreshadowed greatness since this small village was considered a backwater town, a place located near massacres perpetrated by the Roman authorities to deter rebellion. For this and other reasons, Nathanael asked the question in John's Gospel, "Can anything good come from Nazareth" (Jn 1:46).

Based on Matthew's narrative, it is not a stretch of the imagination to conclude that Jesus, who spent his early childhood in Egypt and in the isolated and backwoods town of Nazareth, would speak Aramaic with a Galilean accent that differs from those who grew up in the big city of Jerusalem. This is indirectly confirmed by Peter, a disciple of Jesus, who spoke Aramaic with a Galilean accent and whose hometown was located in Bethsaida in Galilee, only twenty-four miles from Nazareth. In the Passion narrative, after Jesus was arrested and brought before the Sanhedrin, Peter followed Jesus at a distance into the high priest's courtyard. While sitting outside in the courtyard, the bystanders came to Peter and said, "Certainly you too are one of them, for your accent betrays you" (Mt 26:73). Indeed, all the Gospels confirm that Jesus was associated with Nazareth (Mk 1:9; Mt 2:23; Lk 4:16; Jn 1:46). This provides strong evidence that Jesus would have likely sounded like a Galilean in his manner of speech.

What we have thus far is that in Matthew's infancy narrative, we witness the plight of the holy family as refugees. Jesus and his parents were illegal aliens, people without a country. We can assume that he spoke Aramaic with a nonstandard accent, which means that Jesus could identify with the Karen, Hmong, Chin, Vietnamese, and others who came to the United States as refugees. He could identify with the approximately 17,000 Chinese immigrants who came illegally in the late nineteenth and early twentieth centuries by way of Mexico and Canada after the enactment of the Chinese Exclusion Act. He could identify with the immigrant population of the twenty-first century who speak English with an accent or Asian Americans who are seen as less than Americans despite not having an English fluency problem. Jesus knew what it was like to be a foreigner or someone who did not quite fit into the mainstream culture.

One characteristic of being a perpetual foreigner is to have the experience of being laughed at for the way God has made us—the way we look, the way we speak, and the culture in which we were brought up. If we Christians believe that we are created in the image and likeness of God, then to ridicule someone for the way God has created them is to ridicule the very self of God. We can conjecture that Jesus in his formative years was familiar with the pain and hurts that come from being laughed at because we know that the adult Jesus was not immune to being an object of laughter and ridicule. Laughter can express a dimension of consciousness that gives dignity to the human person, but what Jesus experienced, as portrayed in the Gospels, were often the disdainful aspects of human nature in treating others as objects of ridicule and objectification.

In the Passion narrative, when Jesus was before Herod, who questioned Jesus at length, Jesus did not respond. Herod and his soldiers then mocked Jesus and, after clothing him in a glittering garb, sent him back to Pilate. To satisfy the crowd, Pilate proposed to admonish Jesus, which made the crowd become even more violent in their clamoring for crucifixion, shouting, "Away with this man! Release Barabbas to us." Pilate addressed the crowd, wishing to release Jesus, but the crowd cried out all the more, "Crucify him! Crucify him!" (Lk 23:21). Pilate finally gave in to the crowd by releasing Barabbas and handing Jesus over to be crucified. As the soldiers led Jesus away inside the palace, the assembled cohort clothed him with a purple cloak and put a crown of thorns over his head. They struck Jesus and spat on him. They continued to mock him and then took the purple robe off and put his own clothes on him (Mk 15:17–19). The mob of people then ridiculed and laughed at Jesus because they did not believe he was the Messiah. Luke preserves the harshness of the ridicule even further by noting what the crowd said, "Ah ha, if you are the Son of God, come down from that cross. He saved others; let him save himself if he is the Messiah of God, the chosen one" (Lk 23:39–40). Their laughter, however, had an empty ring to it, for it came from their own ignorance and penury.

Laughter is deceptive as it often hides our own sense of inadequacy. We laugh at those greater than us. Euro-Americans laughed at the early Chinese migrants for their smallness of stature, the "strange" queues that they wore, their "unkempt" habits, the food that they ate because it smelled "different"—but they were the ones who built the most difficult stretches of the railroad, who constructed levees, channels, dikes, and ditches in the Sacramento-San Joaquin River delta, who drained the swampland in the Sacramento Delta and turned it "into some of the most productive and fertile farmland in the country."[3] In the development of various corps that required special skills and care, two horticulturalists helped to transform the agricultural industry: Ah Bing who bred the famous Bing cherries (named after him) in Oregon and Lue Gim Cong of Florida who succeeded in growing frost-resistant oranges that could be shipped around the country in large quantities.[4]

The yellow peril stereotype engenders fear that leads to the rise in hate and violence against Chinese and other AAPI population. This is often manifested in racist violence during economic downturns (e.g., anti-Chinese violence in the 1870s), times of tensions and war with an Asian nation-state (e.g., incarceration of Japanese Americans during World War II), and public health crises (e.g., the current COVID pandemic). One sign of yellow peril-ness is when Asian Americans find themselves in a no-win situation or are being victims, blamed for circumstances well beyond their control. When the economy was good and there were ample jobs, thousands of Chinese laborers were hired and received wages lower than those of Whites to help construct the transcontinental railroad and, later, to work in shoe, textile, and cigar factories. In doing so, the Chinese laborers actually raised the standard of living of White Americans. Then, when the economy slowed and entered the Depression of

---

[3] Erika Lee, *The Making of Asian America: A History* (New York: Simon and Schuster, 2015), 74–75.

[4] Ibid., 75.

the 1870s, Chinese workers were blamed for competing unfairly by working for lower wages and with no family to support.[5] The latter was not true as many Chinese laborers sent remittances back to their families in China. The reason there were very few Chinese families in the West had to do with the racist immigration policy that barred them from bringing their wives and families to the United States. They were blamed for problems not of their doing.

When we turn to Jesus, we see an analogous experience. In the final days of his public ministry, the Pharisees were plotting to entrap Jesus by demanding a yes or no answer to a very complex question. Some of the Pharisees and some Herodians were out to maliciously trap Jesus when they posed the question: "Is it lawful to pay the census tax to Caesar or not?" (Mt 22:17). If Jesus said yes, he would alienate most of the people who followed him and for whom tax was an awful burden. If he said, no, the Pharisees and Herodians would accuse him of siding with the militant group, the Zealots, who refused to pay tax to the Romans. Either way, Jesus found himself in a yellow peril-ness of a no-win situation.

Knowing their malice, Jesus asked them to show him the coin used to pay the tax. As they handed him a coin, Jesus questioned them, "Whose image is this and whose inscription?" (Mt 22:20). They were forced to acknowledge that it is "Caesar's." Jesus escaped from their malicious attempt to trick and trap him with a splendid response, "Then repay to Caesar what belongs to Caesar and to God what belongs to God" (Mt 22:22). Jesus challenged them to look beyond the simplistic politics presented by the coin and realize that they were called to embrace a higher set of values rooted in a sacramental consciousness that God is present in all peoples and things.

As they set forth following the stars, the magi consulted with Herod who conferred with the chief priest and scribes regarding

---

[5] Ibid., 74.

where the king was to be born and was told that the Scripture points to Bethlehem of Judea as the birthplace of the Messiah. In response to this news, Herod plotted to kill hordes of infants for fear that one of them would take over his throne. This is the most obvious example that resembles the yellow peril threat. Similarly, after a devastating surprise attack by Japanese Imperial Navy Air Service on a US naval base at Pearl Harbor, Japanese Americans became a yellow peril threat to US national security as President Franklin D. Roosevelt signed the Executive Order 9066 that incarcerated over 100,000 Japanese Americans for fear that they might be working for the Japanese government—even though many were US citizens by birth. In *American Sutra: A Story of Faith and Freedom in the Second World War*, Duncan Ryūken Williams asserts that the religious affiliation of Japanese Americans as Buddhists rendered them vulnerable to racial violence, loss of jobs, properties, and civil liberties.[6]

There are many instances in Scripture where Jesus exhibited the model minority characteristic. The twelve-year-old Jesus who astonished the temple teachers by "his understanding and his answers" (Lk 2:46-47) clearly depicts the teenage Jesus as a "whiz kid," a "model minority." After performing many mighty deeds, including the calming of a storm at sea, the healing of a possessed man at Gerasenes, Jairus's daughter, and a woman with a hemorrhage, Jesus returned to his hometown of Nazareth to teach in the synagogue on the Sabbath. Many were astonished by what he said, but they could not believe that a local boy could be a miracle worker. They were also resentful of his wisdom and achievements. They asked, "Where did this man get all this? What kind of wisdom has been given him? What mighty deeds are wrought by

---

[6] Duncan Ryūken Williams, *American Sutra: A Story of Faith and Freedom in the Second World War* (Cambridge, MA: Harvard University Press, 2019), 27–37.

his hands?" (Mk 6:2). They thought they knew who he was, so they identified Jesus in the family and clan in which he was embedded: "Is he not the carpenter, the son of Mary, and the brother of James and Joses and Judas and Simon? And are not his sisters here with us?" (Mk 6:3). In other words, they took offense at him, saying, we know your origin. You're not a miracle worker. You're the son of a carpenter. They thought they knew who Jesus was, but they did not know him at all.

In the synagogue, Jesus unrolled the scroll handed to him and proclaimed the text of Isaiah against his own background and the needs of the people at his time: "The Spirit of the Lord is upon me, because he has anointed me to bring glad tidings to the poor. He has sent me to proclaim liberty to captives and recovery of sight to the blind, to let the oppressed go free[.]" (Lk 4:18). After his proclamation, Jesus sat down and said, "Today this scripture passage is fulfilled in your hearing" (Lk 4:22). Jesus declared that the Kingdom of God is at hand and the central aspect of this Kingdom is the good news for the poor.

Theological Basis for the Good News for the Poor

The social context that CST foregrounds is the life setting in which the poor find God's presence in their midst. Throughout the Gospels, the centrality of the good news for the poor can be seen in Jesus's proclamation of the advent of the Kingdom of God and the ways in which he reached out to the poor and powerless. The Church, therefore, from its very beginning, has shown active concern for the poor and has provided direct service to the poor and the marginalized in society. Since outreach to the poor is a central part of the Catholic Church's social teaching and ministry, I will further conclude by looking more closely at the theological basis for the good news for the poor and magisterial formulations of a preferential option for the poor.

The late Carroll Stuhlmueller, professor at the Catholic Theological Union and an acclaimed biblical scholar, characterized the Gospel of Luke as the "Gospel of the Poor." In "The Gospel According to Luke," Stuhlmueller noted that "this spirit (i.e., of merciful concern for the poor) shines brightly in the Infancy Narrative, where the poor and insignificant are chosen for the greatest privileges."[7] The poor are special objects of Luke's attention in writing his Gospel.[8] In *New Testament Theology*, Joachim Jeremias provides a framework within which such a linkage seems warranted. For Jeremias, Jesus's words and works constitute his proclamation of salvation, whose central theme is the imminent, sudden onset of the Kingdom of God (*basileia tou theou*) and to the Kingdom the poor have apparently been offered exclusive access.[9]

What makes this proclamation so electrifying is the hope that Jesus held out for those categorically written off as beyond the pale of God's love and, conversely, the offense Jesus gave to those "righteous" ones, the self-styled arbiters of divine love.[10] As presented in the Gospels, the Pharisees, who enjoyed the respect of Palestinian Jewish society at large, had driven a variety of people to despair of God's mercy by repeatedly and publicly pronouncing them to be corrupted sinners, thus bringing them into widespread disrepute.[11] Those whom the Pharisees singled out as sinners included not only robbers, adulteresses, murderers, and other notorious transgressors of the commandments but also gamblers, money lenders, tax

---

[7] Carroll Stuhlmueller, "The Gospel According to Luke," *The Jerome Biblical Commentary*, no. 44:9.

[8] Ibid., no. 44:4, 7.

[9] Joachim Jeremias, *New Testament Theology*, trans. John Bowden (New York: Charles Scribner's Sons, 1971), 96, 101, 102, 107, 108, 116, 121.

[10] Ibid., 113, 116, 118.

[11] Luise Schottroff and Wolfgang Stegemann, *Jesus and the Hope of the Poor*, trans. Matthew J. O'Connell (Maryknoll, NY: Orbis Books, 1986), 89.

collectors, and other individuals whose occupations were tainted by frequent dishonest practices. The same attitude extended to those whose adherence to the Jewish law was wanting.[12]

Jesus, on the other hand, interpreted those same laws differently (Mt 5:17). The message he delivered was addressed to everyone held in contempt by the acknowledged religious leaders of the period. It was transmitted to all who were rendered desolate because of such disabling conditions as indigence, grief, imprisonment, sickness, servitude, and ignorance.[13] This message might be expressed as follows: Since God's loving-kindness is a free gift for all to accept or reject, it cannot be either earned or circumscribed by human effort. The biblical *anawim*, the poor and lowly, are those who admit to their powerlessness in this respect and consign themselves to God's mercy for help in their need. They alone, cognizant of their ultimate sterility, will encounter the unconditional acceptance and forgiveness of God. They will begin to experience deliverance from whatever diminishes their capacity to accept God's gift with gratitude in their hearts. They will assume toward others God's loving stance toward them revealed in Jesus's proclamation of the Kingdom of God.[14]

Preferential Option for the Poor

The preferential option for the poor is one of the newer principles and essential elements of CST. While the expression "preferential option for the poor" originated in Latin American liberation theology, the

---

[12] Jeremias, *New Testament Theology*, 111, 113. Cf. Walter Kasper, *Jesus the Christ*, trans. V. Green (New York: Paulist Press, 1986), 89.

[13] For comments on the focus of Jesus's proclamation in the earliest tradition vis-à-vis the focus found in the Gospel of Luke, see Schottroff and Stegemann, *Jesus and the Hope of the Poor*, 89.

[14] Jeremias, *New Testament Theology*, 117–19. Cf. Leonardo Boff, *Jesus Christ Liberator* (Maryknoll, NY: Orbis Books, 1978), 64, 66, 75–77.

papal magisterium has formulated a new interpretation of the same phrase. In *Gaudium et Spes*, or "Pastoral Constitution on the Church in the Modern World," the Second Vatican Council set the stage for a renewed understanding of the Church's evangelizing mission in society. In his address during the last General Meeting of the Second Vatican Council, Pope Paul VI took an anthropological turn by introducing a new humanism centered on God and Christ.[15] We find this idea continued in his encyclical *Populorum Progressio*, in which Pope Paul VI stated that "this new Christian humanism not only meant struggling for a better world in general but consisted in social concerns for the poor, the disinherited, and developing countries."[16]

The first time "preferential option for the poor" appeared in a Roman document was in *Libertatis Conscientia* under the heading "love of preference for the poor," in the Extraordinary Bishops' Synod of 1985. It emphasizes the love for the poor, the oppressed, and for those whose human rights have been denied. Pope John Paul II used the expression "option or love of preference for the poor" in many of his encyclicals.[17] For Pope Francis, the preferential option for the poor characterized his entire pontificate, one that is connected to "the church's message of inclusion of the poor, advocating for structural reforms that place the human person at the center of the economy and not money."[18]

In Hebrew Scripture, the preferential option for the poor refers to the widows, orphans, and migrants or foreigners, the three most marginalized groups of the time. For the Hebrew prophets,

---

[15] Paul VI, "Address During the Last General Meeting of the Second Vatican Council," December 7, 1965.

[16] Martin Schlag, "The Preferential Option for the Poor and Catholic Social Teaching," in *Catholic Social Teaching: A Volume of Scholarly Essays*, ed. Gerard V. Bradley and E. Christian Brugger (New York: Cambridge University Press, 2019), 469.

[17] Ibid., 470.

[18] Ibid., 478.

the quality of their faith depended on justice in the land. In other words, the moral test of a society depended on how it treated its most vulnerable members. Whether or not the rich and the powerful stand with God depends on whether or not they stand with the marginalized. In ancient Israel, the marginalized were the orphans, widows, and the aliens. And the marginalized people during the New Testament time were the powerless, which included the outsiders, the weak, and the hated underclass: Samaritans, tax collectors, prostitutes, lepers, the poor, the blind, and the neglected.

Throughout the Bible, the poor is not simply a social category, but rather a theological one. In this respect, the poor who encountered God in their lives are usually referred to as the *anawim*, a Hebrew word for "poor and lowly ones," whom Jesus called the blessed poor ones. They are blessed not because they are poor *per se*, but because they are able to recognize their own condition of powerlessness to cope with adversity by sole recourse to their own efforts and thereby place their trust in God.

Today, we need to ask the same question that the prophets did in ancient Israel: How have we treated the poor and most vulnerable members of our society? They have the most urgent claim on our collective conscience. Where a community stands with God depends on where it stands with those on the margins. Among the poor and powerless in the United States today are Blacks, Indigenous, and People of Color (BIPOC). They are today's widows, orphans, strangers, foreigners, or migrants. To be sure, one cannot reify the entire ethnic group as being powerless. Within all these groups, as well as BIPOC, there are the privileged few, in terms of wealth and power, although they may still experience racial microaggressions and even occasional blatant racism in their lives. Moreover, we have to remember that the concept of race, as we understand it today, did not exist during biblical times. The biblical *anawim* are not only those who suffer but also those who remain faithful to God in adversity. Having said that, to determine the character of justice in the twenty-first century, we need to ask the question, how do BIPOC and other powerless people fare among us? The answer to this important question will determine the character of justice.

Principles of Solidarity, the Common Good, and Subsidiarity

The various working committees that drafted responses for the bishops in the production of a pastoral letter and a pastoral response, overlooked the ways in which many elements of CST are already reflected in the practices of community-based organizations. These organizations include Asian Americans Advancing Justice (AAAJ), Asian Pacific Policy and Planning Council, Asian American and Pacific Islander, Chinese for Affirmative Action, Center for the Pacific Asian Family, National Asian Pacific American Women's Forum, and many other AAPI organizations working with the vulnerable and marginalized population in AAPI communities.

During the recent spate of violence against Asian American elders and women, it would not be unreasonable to call for greater police presence to protect the most vulnerable in Asian neighborhoods. Many leaders of community-based organizations, however, cautioned against overreliance on law enforcement and the criminal justice system to address violence, since this can contribute to the criminalization of African Americans in particular. They realized that the best way to protect the most vulnerable was to get to the root of violence in communities of color by working in concert with others who are marginalized. While acknowledging that some of the attackers have been people of color, John C. Yang, president and CEO of AAAJ, called for cross-racial discussions through coalition-building rather than punitive action by advocating for more policing.[19] This idea of not resorting to demonization or scapegoating another community of color and seeking to build a coalition with that community to resolve a problem exemplifies the best of the solidarity principles of CST. This has been demonstrated by a number of public protests and racial peace rallies that emphasized "Black and Asian Solidarity" from San Francisco and Oakland, California, to Union Square, New York City.[20]

A similar approach was taken many centuries ago by Pope Leo the Great who averted the sacking of Rome by using his diplomatic skills rather than violence by meeting with Attila the Hun at the gates of Rome. For this, Leo is known as a peacemaker who knew that violence would lead to more violence and that peacemaking was the way of the antithesis of the Sermon on the Mount. The basic formula for antithesis is, "You have heard and been taught this, but here is what you should actually believe and do." Antitheses are hyperbole. They are exaggerated statements in which Jesus invites his followers to complete fidelity to God's will in all things. In his teaching about retaliation, Jesus said, "You have heard that it was said, 'An eye for an eye and a tooth for a tooth. But I say to you, offer no resistance to one who is evil. When someone strikes you on [your] right cheek, turn the other [one] to him as well (Mt 5:38–39). Jesus was not advising his disciples to let evildoers freely abuse them; rather, he directed them, if possible, not to retaliate by the same violent means. He directed them to respond with an action that confronts the evildoers nonviolently in order to break the cycle of violence and open up a new possibility. AAPI leaders of community-based organizations who advocate against demonizing another community of color and working with them to resolve the

---

[19] Sakshi Venkatraman, "String of Attacks Against Older Asians Leaves Big City Chinatown on Edge," *NBC News*, February 9, 2021.

[20] Kat Moon, "How a Shared Goal to Dismantle White Supremacy Is Fueling Black-Asian Solidarity," *TIME*, March 25, 2021.

common problem of the effects of White supremacy exemplify this nonviolent approach of the antitheses.

This approach transcends the ethics of the rights of the individual, for a commitment to the ethics of the common good. To achieve an effective system of public safety and security in communities of color, people who live in those communities must agree on the common good. This involves social systems and public institutions, including law enforcement, to work in a manner that benefits the most vulnerable.[21] Achieving a common good in a multicultural and multiracial society, however, is more complex as various groups have their own ideas of how to attain it.

For example, many assault victims, store owners whose shops had been robbed or vandalized, and community leaders have asked for a greater police presence in Oakland and San Francisco Chinatowns.[22] On the other side, there are those calling to defund the police not by eliminating law enforcement altogether but by reallocating money from policing to other agencies and community-based organizations that work with people who are homeless and people afflicted with mental health crises. None of these differences in approaches is insurmountable to the establishment of a common good that respects the rights and responsibilities of all, especially the most vulnerable members of society.

In his encyclical, *Gaudium et Spes*, Pope Paul VI defined the common good as "the sum total of social conditions which allow people, either as groups or as individuals, to reach their fulfillment more fully and more easily." It is a sum total of social conditions in which the rights of the individual must be balanced with the value of the common good.

---

[21] Claire Andre and Manuel Velasquez, "The Common Good," Santa Clara University, https://www.scu.edu/mcae/publications/iie/v5n1/common.html.

[22] Venkatraman, "String of Attacks Against Older Asians."

Rather than relying exclusively on the top-down approach of law enforcement and the criminal justice system to ensure public safety, many AAPI community leaders have advocated for a reliance on community-based organizations that have better resources to provide services to AAPI with mental health needs, disabilities, legal, and race-related bias or violence. The introduction of mediating practices to hold perpetrators accountable and the potential benefits of restorative justice to break the cycle of violence, and a community ambassador program where unarmed citizens walk through neighborhoods escorting elders on their errands, walk them to their cars or homes—all reflect the subsidiarity principle that involves social solutions from the bottom up. The allocation of the state resources provided by higher levels, used to support engagements and decision-making by community-based organizations working with the population living in unjust social settings at local levels, reflects the subsidiarity principle at its best.

The Catholic Church, especially in its pastoral letter against racism, simply cannot ignore anti-Asian racism and xenophobia since they are part of the ongoing conversations on racial reckoning in the United States. While AAPI do not share the breadth and depth of oppressions of African and Native Americans, AAPI do share the common experience of being victims of reprehensible policies of the US government toward its non-White population. These indignities resulted in the genocide and forceful assimilation of Native Americans (e.g., the Dawes Act), the chattel slavery of African Americans (e.g., domestic and productive chattels: the ownership of human beings and their offspring as property), the exploitation of Mexican Americans (e.g., Treaty of Guadalupe Hildalgo), and the yellow peril myth that served to encourage lynching and mob violence that led to the 1882 Chinese Exclusion Act.

Because every racial/ethnic group is racialized differently, Asian Americans' racial positioning since the late 1960s is best seen under Ancheta's insider/outsider spectrum centering on citizenship rather than the Black/White binary in which African Americans were denigrated as property and subhuman. The pervasive and destructive stereotypes faced by Asian Americans in the insider/outsider binary are the yellow peril, the model minority, and the forever foreigner. They are part and parcel of our experience that often takes place at levels of subtleties; those who are not part of the experience may not have understood the stereotypes until now, and only by understanding them, and changing them, will full human dignity for Asian Americans according to the ideals of CST become possible.

It is important to tell our stories even if few are listening because our stories are gifts and contributions essential to the fuller understanding of the identity of the Catholic Church and our nation. They are some of the missing pieces necessary for the attainment of authentic racial justice, which cannot be achieved by any one group. The consensus among community organizers, activists, and academics is that solidarity is the best if not the only way to combat racial hatred and violence. For AAPI, this involves building coalitions with Black, Brown, and White allies, bolstering networks of community support, and actively working toward the common good of justice and peace. Although AAPI community-based organizations are not Catholic organizations, the approaches taken by most of these "mediating institutions" that support participation in the process of social change reflect the best of the CST principles: respecting the dignity of every human person, engaging at the local level, and working in solidarity with other racial/ethnic organizations to create a common good of a just society.

Moreover, it is important to tell our stories, some of which may include the pain of marginalization and exclusion, others of which may evoke the deep-felt sense of homelessness and existence. These are the kinds of experiences with which Jesus was familiar in his life. He knew the experience of yellow peril-ness because there was never a time when Jesus's life was not threatened. The synoptic Gospels present Jesus's life as the life of one in peril. He knew what it was like to be a perpetual foreigner. He knew what it was like to speak with a nonstandard accent or to be seen as an outsider. He experienced the pains and hurts that came with being an object of laughter and mocking. Perhaps it was not a coincidence that he made a foreigner the hero in his parable of the Good Samaritan (Lk 10:25–37) or told his disciples not to prohibit another person from casting out demons in his name merely because the man was an outsider (Mk 9:38). Jesus was also a model minority as a successful preacher, teacher, healer, and miracle worker. He served as a model for AAPI because he walked in our shoes and knew what it was like to experience the full range of our humanity. To ignore the experience of AAPI in the ongoing conversation of racial reckoning in the Church and in our nation is to ignore the experience of Jesus himself.

Acknowledgments

As a disturbing trend of violent crimes involving physical assaults on elderly and women of Asian descent has taken place since the start of the COVID-19 pandemic, I have been using my platform to give talks on anti-Asian racism and xenophobia to religious leadership groups, professional organizations, colleges, and universities across the country. An opportunity to put something in writing came when the University of Saint Joseph (USJ) granted me a semester of sabbatical in spring 2021.

As this book was being written, I had the support of many friends and colleagues. I want to express my profound gratitude to Russell Jeung, Janelle Wong, Tammy Ho, Tim Tseng, Jeffrey Burns, John Pawlikowski, Laurie Brink, and Gale Yee. Russell Jeung offered invaluable ideas and resources on Asian American racial reckoning. Despite his hectic schedule with Stop AAPI Hate, and answered all of my emails promptly, even during his vacation. Janelle Wong offered invaluable feedback on theoretical aspects of the Model Minority Myth. Tammy Ho encouraged me and provided instructive feedback on my earliest draft of chapter 1. My heartfelt thanks to Tim Tseng and Jeff Burns for providing invaluable feedback and resources for the historical section of my book; John Pawlikowski for his guidance on the Vatican documents; Laurie Brink and Gale Yee for their perceptive feedback to the biblical section of my volume.

My sincere thanks to Jon Sweeney of Orbis Books who guided this volume to its successful completion with his expert editorial suggestions and comments. My thanks also to Jill O'Brien who provided guidance in the initial stage of this project. My special thanks to Maria Angelini, managing editor at Orbis, who patiently corrected syntax errors in the proofs, and, at times, offered wise comments on the text.

I am grateful for the many support staff at the Pope Pius XII Library of USJ: Kathleen Kelly who secured many books through interlibrary loans; Christina Flood and Ann Williams for providing journal articles and many good ideas about the cover of my book. Thanks also to Lacey Dargenio, a student in my Honors class, who helped me to make the final decision on the cover page of my book.

Last but not least, I am greatly appreciative of Rhona Free, President of USJ, for publicizing my book in both words and writing.

Index